$\mathcal{A}$ COURSE OF
LOVE

THE COURSE OF LOVE SERIES

Book One: *A Course of Love*
Book Two: *The Treatises of A Course of Love*
Book Three: *The Dialogues of A Course of Love*

A COURSE OF
LOVE

COURSE OF LOVE PUBLICATIONS
ST. PAUL, MINNESOTA

Course of Love Publications
432 Rehnberg Place
W. St. Paul, Minnesota 55118
www.acourseoflove.com
acol@thedialogues.com

First Course of Love Publications Edition.
Printed in the United States of America.
Originally published by New World Library, Novato, CA, 2001.

The Library of Congress has classified the
hardcover edition of this book as follows:
1. Love—Religious aspects—Christianity. 2. Christian life.

ISBN 0-9728668-2-5

This edition is printed on 60 lb. Vellum natural recycled paper.

Distributed in the United States by Itasca Books
Prism Publishing Center
5120 Cedar Lake Road
Minneapolis, MN 55416
www.ItascaBooks.com

*T*his is a call to move now into my embrace
and let yourself be comforted.
Realize that this is the whole world,
the universe, the all of all
in whose embrace you literally exist.

Feel the gentleness and love.
Drink in the safety and the rest.
Close your eyes and begin to see
with an imagination
that is beyond thought and words. . . .

Our heart is the light of the world.

— *A Course of Love* 20.2–4

SUBSTANTIVE CHANGES to the
SECOND EDITION

*T*he second edition of *A Course of Love* includes a new foreword. Also "new" is a return to the original language of the text as it was received. In the first edition, published by New World Library in 2001, language was removed that referred to this work directly as a continuation of the work begun in *A Course of Miracles*. Since the first printing, copyright concerns have been resolved; therefore, the original language has been restored.

In a new addendum, "Learning in the Time of Christ," Jesus speaks of a way of "taking" this Course without learning or study. Excerpts are included in this edition. The full text is available from the website: www.acourseoflove.com.

The remaining changes are of deletions rather than additions. The intent of these changes is to leave only the essential. The introduction and comments made by early supporters of the Course are preserved on the Course of Love website.

CONTENTS

LEARNING in the TIME of CHRIST

FOREWORD

The first section of this foreword was given by Jesus. The second was written by Mari Perron who received the text of the Course of Love series.

This course was written for the mind — but only to move the mind to appeal to the heart. To move it to listen. To move it to accept confusion. To move it to cease its resistance to mystery, its quest for answers, and to shift its focus to the truth and away from what can be learned only by the mind.

What is learned by the mind only rearranges reality. The mind then holds to the new reality as a new set of rules without change. It sees reality through these new mental constructs and calls this way of seeing new. In order to support its new reality it must insist that others follow these new rules. Truth, it says, has been found, and it is "here" in these new rules and not in those of old. The mind will then tell you how to feel according to its rules and will resist all ways of feeling, all ways of being, that appear to run counter to these rules, as if it knows, because of these rules, how things are.

The mind will speak of love and yet hold the heart prisoner to its new rules, new laws, and still say "this is right" and "this is wrong." It will speak of love and not see its intolerance or judgment. It will speak of love to be helpful and with all sincerity, and yet the very logic that it uses, though new, wounds the heart of the most tender, of those most called to love and its sweetness. "I am wrong to feel the way I do" the tender-hearted says to herself and, convinced that another knows what she does not, covers-over her tenderness with protection.

You think that in order to share you must be able to speak the same language and so you regress to the language of the mind with its precision. The mind so hates to be confused, to be open, to remain open, and to not know. It desires anchors to hold it in one spot, and held there suffers the pounding of the sea of change, resists the current, fortifies itself against the storm. The mind will return always to where it feels safe and sure of itself and so it goes nowhere and sees not transformation, or creation, or the new horizon that would defy its reality.

The mind cannot hold open the doors of the heart and yet we turn within, turn to the mind, and show it where its openness lies, where sweetness abides, where love's knowing is found. All the mind can do is rearrange reality and hold it still and captive and rule bound. The laws of love are not laws such as these. The laws of love are not rules, facts, or right answers. The laws of love bring spiritual freedom, the freedom that lies beyond belief, beyond thought, beyond adherence to any authority other than one's own heart.

The heart is needed to guide the mind in a way that it does not desire to be guided, a way that is one of joining, a way that does not allow the mind's separate stance, its rules, or its right answers. The heart is needed because it is who and where you are and responds in love to what is one with it. We are one heart.

We are one mind. The route to oneness and union, to life in form that accepts oneness and union, to a humanity restored to wholeness, is through the heart of the mind.

This Course will seem remedial to some, easy to some, complex to some. The mind may say, "Yes, yes, I know. Tell me some-

thing I don't know." The mind may reel at contradictions, cling to known truths, compare this wisdom to other wisdom. The mind will attempt to understand with its own logic and fight the logic of the heart. The mind will seek new rules and perhaps be willing to rearrange its reality once again.

The mind is its own reality. You cannot escape the mind's reality with the mind. You cannot learn how to escape the reality of the mind with the mind's pattern of learning or of logic. You cannot live in a new and fresh world and retain the mind's reality.

There is no "everyone" to whom I speak, to whom I give these words. There is no single, no solitary, no separate mind to whom these words are spoken. These words are spoken heart to heart, from One Heart to One Heart.

"Everyone" is just a concept. These words are given to each One. They are heard only by each "alone" by which I mean in the sanctity of the One Heart. We are one heart. We are one mind. Joined in wholeheartedness we are the heaven of the world. We replace bitterness with sweetness. We dwell in the reality of the One Heart, creation's birthplace, birthplace of the new.

The new is not that which has always existed. It is not that which can be predicted. It is not that which can be formed and held inviolate. The new is creation's unfolding love. The new is love's expression. The new is the true replacement of the false, illusion's demise, joy birthed amongst sorrow. The new is yet to be created, One Heart to One Heart.

This is a course for the heart. The birthplace of the new.

MARI PERRON, FEBRUARY 14, 2006

In *A Course of Love,* as well as in *A Course in Miracles*, Jesus says that love cannot be taught. What can't be taught is a mystery. These messages from Jesus are both mystery and revelation of mystery.

In 1998, I was reading *A Course in Miracles* and seeking my own heart's calling when I heard a Voice tell me that I would receive a new course in miracles. As you might imagine, my part in this mystery — having this Course of Love come to me and through me — raised a number of questions.

How did it happen? How was this guidance made possible? What did I actually experience?

Receiving Jesus and his guidance was easy. I loved the relationship and the process by which I wrote. The words arose from within, more-or-less as thoughts I didn't think. This writing practice lasted three years. The work of it was effortless, uncomplicated, and awe-inspiring.

There was a way I made it difficult though. This is what I want to tell you about. This difficulty showed me something, and may show you something, about the *newness* Jesus calls us to in asking us to give up our struggles.

It was when each day's writing was done that difficulty would arise. That was when I would begin to think about it. Thinking about it, I felt overwhelmed. My mind struggled and grew painfully frustrated by its inability to comprehend what was happening and even what was being said. My mind could not accept the new experience. I couldn't understand it, explain it, or compare it to anything else.

My feelings fared little better. As soon as I stood back from the work I was doing, I felt like a peon on an iceberg enveloped by immensity. I felt surrounded by the most powerful force in the universe, as if I was in the eye of a hurricane.

Yet I was just sitting at my desk. A mere moment away from dinner. I'd find it hard to believe I could still eat. Hearing the sound of the television or the phone ringing would whisk me back from my iceberg in a nanosecond. The shift in atmosphere felt as if it would just about kill me.

I knew I couldn't continue to feel union only when I was actively engaged in the work. I couldn't continue to feel miserable as soon as it stopped. I reasoned that if I could only get a clear grasp, a definitive understanding of what was going on, then I would "have it." I could "achieve" lasting union. I kept trying to make this experience be like other experiences I had learned from and learned to duplicate — experiences from which I had always stood back — a mind, or a self, observing.

It wasn't by the *effort* of my mind, but through *stillness* of mind, that I eventually realized that it wasn't something miraculous about "the work" that made union possible and separation intolerable. Union was what arose naturally when the blocks to my awareness of love's presence were removed. That was what happened as I received this Course. The barrier of my separate thoughts melted away and Jesus was with me without being "other than me." We were in relationship without being separate.

In union there is no "self" standing back, observing the experience. Without a separate consciousness, there is no thought. Without thought there is oneness of being.

When I saw this, I knew that I could experience oneness in life, that I'd had these experiences in the past, and that I continue to have them. They just weren't experiences of my thinking mind.

It would only be *after* such an experience that an awareness that "something happened" would come. Then I'd think, *Oh my God, that was the greatest thing ever. I want to have that again.* Once more the work would begin toward realizing unity wasn't something I could "have" and that it's who I am when I'm not being an "other" to myself; when I'm not being separate.

When I'm thinking, I'm present to this "other" who is

the self I think I am. "She" is there in my thoughts just like any other person, thing, or situation taking up space in my mind. I am not alone with God and not in unity.

Having an "I," and all that is not "I," is the way of thinking. This is *not* the way of the heart that Jesus calls us to. He ends this Course by saying "Think not."

To move from the experience of separation to the experience of union, is to experience the power of God and the force of love. It is an unthinkable experience.

Jesus says, *Start with this idea: You will allow for the possibility of a new truth to be revealed to your waiting heart. Hold in your heart the idea that as you read these words — and when you finish reading these words — their truth will be revealed to you. Let your heart be open to a new kind of evidence of what constitutes the truth.* 7.23

Revelation is what this Course is, as well as the new way of knowing that it invites. When I received *A Course of Love* I received revelation. When I thought about it, I blocked my ability to recognize what I received.

You are about to receive this Course. As you open your heart to Jesus, let him, rather than your mind, lead the way. When you close the book and go about your day, hold it in your heart. Stay in love's presence. Allow yourself to quit standing back from life, a separate self. Start at the beginning, with who you truly are. Don't think too much. Let your heart recognize what it receives. Then you will see that . . .

In the beginning, and before the beginning, and before the before, there was only love. . . .

$\mathcal{A}$ COURSE OF
LOVE

THE PRELUDE

You have traveled your path and the end of the journey is in sight. You stand at the precipice with a view of the new world glittering with all the beauty of heaven set off at just a little distance in a golden light. — P.16

This is a course in miracles. It is a required course. The time P.1
for you to take it is now. You are ready and miracles are needed.

Pray for all those in need of miracles. To pray is to ask. But P.2
for what are you asking? This is the first instruction in this
course in miralces. All are in need of miracles. This is the
first step in miracle readiness: asking for all to be included in
what we do here. By praying for all those in need of miracles
you are praying for all to learn as you learn, you are asking
to link your mind with all minds. You are asking to end your
separated state and learn in a state of unity. This is a basic
recognition that this is the only way you learn.

The separated self or the ego does not learn. Even when the P.3
ego has taken many courses and received many teachings,
the ego has not learned but has merely become threatened.
Spirit does not need a course in miracles. If the ego cannot learn and the spirit does not need to, then who is this
Course and all other such courses for? Learning our true
identity, the identity of the Self that is capable of learning, is something everyone must do. Can the ego learn

xxi

this? Never. Does spirit need to? No. Who, then, is this course for?

P.4   This is a basic question that was not adequately answered in *A Course in Miracles.* While a course in miracles is meaningless to the ego and unnecessary to spirit it would seem to have no audience at all if these are the only two states that exist. Since it is impossible to be part spirit and part ego, assuming there would be such a state in which learning could take place would be meaningless.

P.5   The world as a state of being, as a whole, has entered a time, brought on largely by *A Course in Miracles,* in which readiness for miracle-mindedness is upon it. *A Course in Miracles* opened a door by threatening the ego. All those who, with egos weakened, walked this world with the hope of leaving ego behind, with miracle-minded intent, have awakened human beings to a new identity. They have ushered in a time of ending our identity crisis. Not since Jesus walked the earth has such a time been upon humankind.

P.6   What is it in you that is capable of learning? What is it in you that recognizes that ego is not what you are? What is it in you that recognizes your spirit? What is it in you that hovers between two worlds, the world of the ego's dominion and that of spirit? What recognizes the difference? The Christ in you.

P.7   It is easy to imagine how the Christ in you differs from your ego but not as easy to recognize how the Christ in you differs from spirit. The Christ in you is that which is capable of learning in human form what it means to be a child of God. The Christ in you is that which is capable of bridging the two worlds. This is what is meant by the second coming of Christ.

The ego is what you made. Christ is what God made. The ego is your extension of who you think you are. Christ is God's extension of who He is. In order to end the need for learning, you must know who you are and what this means. Where the original Course in Miracles was a course in thought reversal and mind training, a course to point out the insanity of the identity crisis and dislodge the ego's hold, this is a course to establish your identity and to end the reign of the ego. P.8

There are still few who dare to believe in the glory of who they are, few who can lay aside the idea that to think of themselves in the light of God's thought of them rather than their own is arrogance. This is only because the ego is not yet and finally gone. You are right not to desire to glorify the ego in any way. You know that the ego cannot be glorified and that you would not want it to be. This is why, while the ego remains, you cannot know who you are. The only glory is of God and His creations. That you are among the creations of God cannot be disputed. Thus all glory is due you. All glory is yours, and your efforts to protect it from the ego's reach are valiant but unnecessary. The ego cannot claim the glory that is yours. P.9

Many of you desire to be "foot soldiers," to just live the good life without claiming glory, without having any grand ideas about yourselves. It is possible to do much good without recognizing who you are, but it is impossible to be who you are, and you are what the world is for. Your recognition of your Self and your recognition of your brothers and sisters is what the world is for. To stop before this is accomplished when it is in reach is every bit as insane as belief in the ego. Ask yourself what it is that stops you. As humble as you seem to be in your choice, you are still letting ego make your choice. This is not humility but fear. P.10

P.11 The further teachings of the original Course were designed to turn fear into love. When you think you can go only so far and no further in your acceptance of the teachings of the Course and the truth of yourself as God created you, you are abdicating love to fear. You are perhaps making this world a better place but you are not abolishing it. In your acceptance of doing good works and being a good person, you are accepting ministry to those in hell rather than choosing heaven. You accept what you view as possible and reject what you perceive as impossible. You thus cling to the laws of man and reject the laws of God. You claim your human nature and reject your divine nature.

P.12 What is this rejection but rejection of yourself? What is this rejection but fear masquerading as humility? What is this rejection but rejection of God? What is this but a rejection of miracles?

P.13 You who have rejected yourself are likely to feel increasingly burdened. Although an initial burst of energy may have followed your reading of the Course or your discoveries of other forms of the truth, although you may even have experienced what seemed to be miracles happening "to" you, as you continued to reject yourself, this energy and these experiences that lightened your heart would have begun to recede and to seem as distant and unreal as a mirage. All that you retain is a belief in effort and struggle to be good and to do good, a belief that clearly demonstrates that you have rejected who you are.

P.14 Oh, Child of God, you have no need to try at all, no need to be burdened or to grow tired and weary. You who want to accomplish much good in the world realize that only you can be accomplished. You are here to awaken from your slumber. You are here not to awaken to the same world, a world that seems a little more sane than before but still governed by insanity, a world in which it seems possible to help a few others but certainly not all others, but to awaken to a new world. If all that you see changed within your world is a little less insanity than before, then you have not awakened but still are caught in the nightmare your ego has made. By choosing to reject yourself you have chosen to try to make sense of the nightmare rather than to awaken from it. This will never work.

By rejecting who you are, you are demonstrating that you think you can believe in some of the truth but not all of it. Many of you have accepted, for instance, that you are more than your body while retaining your belief in the body. You thus have confused yourself further by accepting that you are two selves — an ego self represented by the body and a spirit self that represents to you an invisible world in which you can believe but not take part. You thus have placed the ego at odds with spirit, giving the ego an internal and invisible foe to do battle with. This was hardly the purpose of the Course or of any teachings of the truth that have as their aim the exact opposite of this conflict-inducing situation. The truth unites. It does not divide. The truth invites peace, not conflict. Partial truth is not only impossible, it is damaging. For sooner or later in this lopsided battle, the ego will win out. The spirit as you have defined it is too amorphous, too lacking in definition and believability to win this battle against what you perceive as your reality. ^{P.15}

You who have come close to truth only to turn your back and refuse to see it, turn around and look once again. You have traveled your path and the end of the journey is in sight. You stand at the precipice with a view of the new world glittering with all the beauty of heaven set off at just a little distance in a golden light. When you could have seen this sight you turned your back and sighed, looking back on a world familiar to you, and choosing it instead. You do not see that this ^{P.16}

choice, even made with every good intention of going back and making a difference, is still a choice for hell when you could instead have chosen heaven. Yet you know that choosing heaven is the only true way to change the world. It is the exchange of one world for another. This is what you fear to do. You are so afraid to let go of the world that you have known that, even though it is a world of conflict, sickness, and death, you will not exchange it, will not relinquish it.

P.17   While God remains unknown to you and you remain unknown to yourself, so too does heaven remain concealed. Thus, in turning your back on heaven, you turn your back on your Self and God as well. Your good intentions will not overcome the world and bring an end to hell. In all the history of the world, many have done good, heroic, and at times miraculous deeds without the world changing from a place of misery and despair. What is more arrogant? To believe that you alone can do what millions of others have not been able to do? Or to believe that you, in union with God, can? What makes more sense? To choose to try again what others have tried and failed to accomplish? Or to leave behind the old and choose a new way, a way in which you become the accomplished, and in your accomplishment bring the new into being?

P.18   What is the difference between your good intentions and willing with God? The difference is in who you think you are and who God knows you to be. While this difference remains you cannot share your will with God or do what God has appointed you to do. Who you think you are reveals the choice that you have made. It is either a choice to be separate from God or a choice to be one with God. It is a choice to know yourself as you always have, or a choice to know your Self as God created you. It is the difference between wanting to know God now, and wanting to wait to know God until you have decided you are worthy or until some other designated time, such as at death.

What are good intentions but a choice to do what you can, P.19 alone, by yourself, against great odds? This is why good intentions so often fail to come to be at all, and why, when every effort has been made, the outcome seldom seems worth the effort. You cannot earn your way to heaven or to God with your effort or your good intentions. You cannot earn, and will not ever feel as if you have earned, the designation of a person of such worth that you are deserving of all that God would freely give. Give up this notion.

You have decided that you know how to do good works P.20 but that you do not know how to do what God asks of you. You think, if God asked me to build a bridge I would build a bridge, and this is likely true. Yet you will not become the bridge. You refuse to recognize that the Christ in you provides the bridge that you need only walk across to close the distance between heaven and hell, between your separated self and union with God and all your brothers and sisters. You prefer to think a good deed here, a bit of charity there, is more important. You prefer to give up on yourself and to help others, without realizing that you can help no others until you have helped yourself. You prefer selflessness to self because this is your chosen way to abolish ego and to please God. This is not unlike the attitude of a good mother who decides to sacrifice herself for her children, without realizing that her sacrifice is not only unnecessary but undesirable.

Your good intentions neither please nor displease God. God P.21 simply waits for your return to heaven, for your acceptance of your birthright, for you to be who you are.

P.22   Another failure to accomplish lies at the other end of the spectrum, with a concentration on self that seems to have no end point and no limit to the interest it generates. While forgiveness and the release of guilt are necessary, and while recognition of gifts and what leads to joy cannot be done without, the point of these essential teachings is only to make one ready for a new choice. Prolonged interest in self can be as damaging as the selflessness of those intent on doing good works. Rather than leading to knowledge of God, prolonged interest in self can further entrench the ego.

P.23   Seekers are but another category of those who at the precipice act as if they have hit a wall rather than come across a bridge. It is precisely the place at which you stopped that you must return to. Those who continue to seek may have left teachings of the Course or of one or another spiritual or religious tradition only to find another and still another. For those intent on seeking there is always more to seek, but those who find must stop to realize what they have found and to realize that they seek no more.

P.24   The Course speaks of patience that is infinite. God is patient but the world is not. God is patient for God sees you only as you are. The Christ in you is also still and ever present. But the weakening done your ego by whatever learning you have done has left room for strength, a strength that entered as if by a little hole made in your ego's armor, a strength that grows, and grows impatient with delay. It is not your ego that grows impatient for change, for your ego is highly invested in things remaining the same. It is, rather, a spirit of compassion that reels at the senselessness of misery and suffering. A spirit that seeks to know what to do, a spirit that does not believe in the answers it has been given.

The way to overcome the dualism that threatens even the most P.25 astute of learners is through the Christ in you, through the One who knows what it is to be God's child and also to walk the earth as child of man. This is not your helper, as the Holy Spirit is, but your identity. While the Holy Spirit was properly called upon to change your perception and show you the false from the true, your recognition of the Christ in you is proper in this time of identification of your undivided Self.

Let us, for the moment, speak of the family of God in terms P.26 of the family of man, in terms, in short, that you will recognize. In the family of man, there are many families but it is called one family, the family of man. It is called one species, the human species. Within this family of man are individual families, and among them, that which you call "your" family. A family has many members but it is called one family. All of its members are descended from the same ancestors, the same bloodline. Within that bloodline are genes that carry particular traits and predispositions. A child of one family may resemble the child of another distant relative or a relative who lived and died many years previously. You see nothing odd or foreign in this. This is the nature of family, as you understand family. And beyond the physical nature of families, the bloodlines and the ancestors, what holds the family together as one is love. The family is, in fact, the only place where unconditional love is seen as acceptable. Thus, no matter how good one child is perceived to be and how bad another is perceived to be, the love of the parent for the child is the same. A son or daughter does not earn the love that is given him or her, and this too is seen as acceptable and even "right."

Obviously the nature of God is different than the nature of P.27 man. God does not have physical form and does not produce physical offspring. God does, however, have a son, a child, an offspring, who must exist in some form like unto the Father. Within the story of the human race there is a story about the coming of God's son, Jesus Christ, who was born, grew into a man, died, and rose again to live on in some form other than that of a man. Those who believe the story have accepted that Jesus was God's son before he was born, while he walked the earth, and after he died and resurrected. Whether this is your belief or not, it comes close to the truth in a form that you can understand. Jesus is simply the example life, the life that demonstrated what it means to be God's child.

P.28   Just as there is part of you that thinks that you are undeserving and made for suffering and strife, there is another part of you that knows this is not true. Think back, and you will remember that from the earliest of ages you have known that life is not as it appears to be, not even as it is meant to be, and that you are not as you appear to be, not even as you are meant to be. The part of you that rages against injustice, pain, and horror does so from a place that does not accept and will never accept that these things are what are meant for you or for those who walk this world with you. And yet your history, in which you so believe, will tell you that the world has always been thus and that there is no escape from it. In such a world the question should not be why do so many take their lives, but why do so few.

P.29   There are many forms of pain and horror, from physical illnesses to torture to loss of love, and in between these many frightful occurrences is the equally distressing life of the purposeless, where hours pass endlessly in toil that is the cost of your survival here. Even those who have studied much and learned the lessons of the Course well, leave their learning and their teaching sit idly by while they earn their living until the dust that has collected upon it obscures it from their sight.

This is the cost of turning back when heaven could have been reached, the cost in continuing to believe in the laws of the world that govern the survival of the body. This is the way of those who know this is not the way it is meant to be and then doubt their knowing. This is the way it has always been, they cry. They lament that they see but one real world while heaven waits just beyond their willingness to proceed.

You are the creation like unto your Father and the family of P.30 man is like unto the family of God. Just as children grow in your "real world" and leave their family, separate from their family to begin their "own" life, so have you done as part of God's family. In the human family the separateness and independence that come with age are seen as the way that things should be, and yet a return to the "family of origin" is also seen as natural. Children go away for a time, eager to assert their independence, only later to return. The return is the symbol of maturity, acceptance, and often of forgiveness.

What does it mean to believe in God? You recognize that P.31 you cannot know God in the same way in which you know another human being, and yet you keep seeking this type of knowing. However, even with another human being, the essence of knowing them is knowing what they stand for, what their truth is, what rules they obey, how they think and how what they think aligns with what they do. God gave you the Word to know him by. God gave you the word made flesh as an example to live by — an example of a living God. What more than this is necessary? You seek form when you already have content. Does this make any sense?

You read what authors write and feel that you know not only P.32 their characters, but the authors as well. Yet you meet an author face to face and you can seldom see in them what you saw in their writing. When you meet an author face to face, you view their form. When you read their words, you view their content. When you quit seeing with the ego's eyes, you quit seeing form and quit searching for form. You begin seeing content.

P.33   Content is all you have of God. There is no form to see, yet in the content is the form revealed. This is true seeing. For content is all and form is nothing.

P.34   The content of God is love. Jesus embodied God by embodying love. He came to reverse the way God was thought of, to put an end to seeing God in human terms of vengeance, punishment, and judgment.

P.35   Jesus did this not only by embodying God in human form, but by giving a true rather than a false picture of power. Before the coming of the word made flesh, the incarnation, the only idea humankind could draw of an all-powerful being was a being whose power resembled the powerful among them. Jesus took such a stand against those with this kind of power that he was put to death. But Jesus did not abdicate for a powerless people. Jesus taught true power, the power of love, a power proven by the resurrection.

P.36   Jesus, united with the Christ in you, can teach you who you are and how to live as who you are in a new world. He can open heaven to you and walk you through its gates, there to exchange this world at last for your true home. But it is not your body that will pass through heaven's gates, nor your body's eyes that will view the new world you will behold and take with you. To view a physical world of dimension, shape, and scope like unto the old and hope to transport it from one place to another would be delusional. The new world does not have to do with form, but with content. A content that is as transferable as an author's words upon a page.

How many would not travel to heaven if they could get P.37 on a bus and be transported there? Yet each of you holds within you the power to reach heaven. Knowing yourself as who you really are is the only thing that will allow you to quit fearing your power. Jesus accepted his power and so brought the power of heaven to earth. This is what the Christ in you can teach you to do. This is miracle-mindedness. This is love.

This is oneness. The Christ in you teaches only in the sense P.38 of imparting knowledge that you already have and once again have access to as you join with your own real Self. Once this is accomplished, you are accomplished. Because you are complete. But if your joining with Christ is the accomplishment and completion of all lessons, who is he who provides the lessons? This is Jesus.

The Christ in you is your shared identity. This shared iden- P.39 tity made Jesus one with Christ. The two names mean the same thing, as oneness is what was always shared and always will be. You are eternally one with Christ. The only way you can identify Jesus differently is to relate to the Jesus who was a man, the Jesus who existed in history. This is the same way in which you are able to see yourself — as man or woman, as a being existing in a particular time in history. This one- or at best three-dimensional nature of your seeing is the nature of the problem. If you cannot see yourself as "other than" a man or woman living in a particular place in a particular time, you cannot see your Self. Thus Jesus comes to you again, in a way that you can accept, to lead you beyond what you can accept to what is true.

To tell someone, even a young child, that a caterpillar P.40 becomes a butterfly is seemingly unbelievable. This does not make it any less true. The butterfly, although some perceive it as being lovelier to behold, is still the same being as the caterpillar. The caterpillar did not cease to exist; it simply transformed into what it always was. Thus it would seem as if the butterfly is both butterfly and caterpillar, two separate things becoming one. You are well aware of the fact that if you could not see the transformation take place "with your own two eyes," you would not believe that the two seemingly disparate creatures were the same. Someone telling you this story of transformation without being able to show you proof that you could see would be accused of making up a fairy tale for your amusement.

P.41 How many of you see the story of your own Self in this same frame of mind? It is a nice fairy tale, an acceptable myth, but until your body's eyes can behold the proof, this is what it will remain. This is the insanity of the nightmare you choose not to awaken from. It is as if you have said I will not open my eyes until someone proves to me that they will see when they are opened. You sit in darkness awaiting proof that only your own light will dispel.

P.42 Your willingness to learn is evident or you would not be here. You have been told and told again that a little willingness is all that is necessary. Why do you seem then to have not advanced or to have advanced only a little bit, when your willingness is mighty? Only because you have not vanquished the ego. You learn and then you let the ego come and take all you have learned from you again and still again. It is ingenious in its ways of getting you to turn back again and still again, until you feel as if you are going in and out through a revolving door.

P.43 You were your Self before you began your learning, and the ego cannot take your Self from you but only can obscure it. Thus the teachings you need now are to help you separate the ego from your Self, to help you learn to hear only one voice.

This time we take a direct approach, an approach that seems P.44 at first to leave behind abstract learning and the complex mechanisms of the mind that so betray you. We take a step away from intellect, the pride of the ego, and approach this final learning through the realm of the heart. This is why, to end confusion, we will call this course *A Course of Love.*

A choice for love creates love. A choice for fear creates fear. What choice do you think has been made to create the world you call your home? This world was created by your choice, and a new world can be created by a new choice. But you must realize that this is all there is. Love or lack of love. Love is all that is real. — 1.18

Every living being has a heart. Let us define heart as the center of being, that place from which all feeling arises. All true feeling is love. All love praises God. All love is recognition of the glory of God and all God created. Love is the only pure response of the created for the creator, the only response of the creator to the created. Your recognition of what love is will return you to God and your Self.   1.1

You learned in *A Course of Miracles* that all knowledge is generalizable. So is feeling. All feeling results from love or lack of love. There are no other reasons for the feelings that you experience. All feelings are generated by the heart and have nothing to do with the body. The heart of the body is the altar at which all your offerings to God are made. All offerings are love or lack of love. Lack of love is nothing. Thus, all offerings made from a place other than love are nothing. All offerings made from a place of fear or guilt are nothing.   1.2

Love is the condition of your reality. In your human form your heart must beat for the life of your self to take place. This is the nature of your reality. Love is as essential to your   1.3

being as the heart to the body. Thus you would not exist without love. It is there even if you are as unaware of it as you are of the beating of your heart. A baby is no less alive because it does not realize its heart is beating. You are no less your Self even though you do not realize that without love you would not exist.

1.4 God's only thought is love. It is a thought without limit, endlessly creating. Because of the extension of God's thought of love, you exist. I exist with you in this self same thought. You do not understand this only because you do not understand the nature of your own thoughts. You have placed them inside your body, conceptualizing them in a form that makes no sense.

1.5 Yet when you apply your thought to learning you learn. Let this encourage you. This is an ability we can use together to learn anew.

1.6 You should be in a hurry only to hear the truth. Of course all of the ways that you act when you want to hurry are contrary to what you would achieve. Let your worries come and let your worries go. Remember always that they simply do not matter except in terms of time, and that you will save time by letting them go. Remember that your worries affect nothing. You think if your worries affect time this is an effect, but time is an illusion. It too does not matter. Remind yourself of this as well. This is part of letting go of the old world to make way for the new. Realize these things do not matter and will not be carried with you to the new world. So you might as well let them go now.

1.7 It is as if you have carried your heavy luggage with you everywhere just in case you might need something. Now you are beginning to trust that you will not need these things you have carried. Ah, no heavy coat is necessary, for you trust the sun will shine, and that warmth will surround you. You are an immigrant coming to a New World with all your possessions in hand. But as you glimpse what was once a distant shore and now is near, you realize none of what you formerly possessed and called your treasures are needed. How silly you feel to have carted them from one place to the next. What a waste of time and energy to have been slowed down by such a heavy burden. What a relief to realize that you need carry it no more. How you wish you would have believed they were not needed when you began. How happy you are to leave them behind.

You do not realize as yet how heavy was your burden. Had 1.8 you literally carried a heavy and useless trunk from one world to another when you had been told by someone wiser that it would not be needed, you would upon realizing the truth ask yourself what else you had been told and disregarded. You might try one more thing and then another that you previously would not have tried when you were so convinced that you were right and the other wrong. And as each new step is tried and found to work, your confidence in the wisdom of this teacher would continue to grow. You might consider that you could still learn from your mistakes and find the learning in the end to be the same, and this you surely might do from time to time. But eventually you would realize that it would be quicker and easier to learn without mistakes, and eventually you would realize also that the wisdom of your teacher had become your own.

The urge to test another's wisdom is the urge to find your 1.9 own way and have it be a better way. It is the urge not to trust the teacher in all things but only in certain things. It is the desire to find your way on your own so that you can take pride in your accomplishment, as if by following another's map the sense of accomplishment in your arrival would be diminished. This wanting to do things on your own is a trick of the ego, your pride a gift the ego demands. These are the magic thoughts that oppose miracle-mindedness. These are the thoughts that say "on my own" I am everything, rather than on my own I am nothing. Those who are true leaders follow until they are ready to lead. They do not strike out on their own at the beginning, before they know the way. There is no shame in learning, no shame in following the course another has put forth. Each true course changes in application. Fifty students may be taught the same lessons and not one will learn in exactly the same way as another. This is true with the teaching and learning of information, and true with the teaching and learning of the truth as well. The only way that you can fail to learn the truth is to demand to learn it on your own. For on your own it is impossible to learn.

1.10   Resign as your own teacher. Accept me as your teacher and accept that I will teach you the truth. Find no shame in this. You cannot learn what I would teach you without me. You have tried in countless ways and can try still again. But you will not succeed — not because you are not smart enough, not because you will not try hard enough, but because it is impossible. It is impossible to learn anything on your own. Your determination to do so only blocks your learning. It is only through union with me that you learn because it is only in union with me that you are your Self. All your effort is based on disbelief of this truth, and your attempts to prove that this truth is not the truth. All that this effort brings you is frustration. All your seeming success from this effort brings you is pride to offer to your ego. This gift your ego demands is not worth the price you pay, for the price of this gift is everything.

A teacher always has a role in the learning of the student.   1.11
This does not diminish the student's achievement. You must
realize it is your desire to make of yourself your own creator
that has caused all your problems. This is the authority
problem. It is pervasive in the life of your physical form and
in the life of your mind. It is only your heart that does not
consider this an issue of concern. This is another reason we
appeal to the heart.

The heart cares not where love comes from, only that it   1.12
comes. This is useful to us in several ways. By this I do not
mean that there are not particular objects of your affection.
This is not the love of which we speak. The heart yearns for
what is like itself. Thus love yearns for love. To think of
achieving love "on one's own" is ludicrous. This is why love
is your greatest teacher. To yearn for what is like yourself is
to yearn for your creator and, when perception is healed, to
create like your creator. This yearning exists naturally within
you and cannot be diminished or satiated.

Those who are seen as loveless and alone in the world are   1.13
those you find to be the objects of your pity. Yet you do not
realize that this is the state your ego has you endlessly striving to achieve. Your ego would have you believe that only
when you need no one to achieve all you desire, only when
you are satisfied with what you are and with what you can
do *on your own,* only then will your autonomy and your
learning be complete, for this is all your learning has been
for. The goal of this world is for you to stand on your own,
complete within yourself. This goal will never be reached,
and only when you give up trying to reach it can you begin
to learn anything of value. You are complete only within
God, where you endlessly abide. Striving to be that which
you can never be is the hell you have created.

1.14   Lack of striving is seen as a settling for less. This would be true if what you were striving for had value. To strive mightily for nothing is still to have nothing and to end up with nothing. Striving, however, must be distinguished from struggle. To strive for that which has value is what this course is about. It has nothing to do with struggle. You think also that to leave struggle behind, to disengage from the conflict of this world that causes it, is to turn your back on the real world and all that has meaning in it. In this you think correctly. And yet you do not choose this option thinking that to do so you turn your back on responsibility and on duty, thus counting this action as a noble one. This desire to engage in struggle has nothing to do with your sense of responsibility and duty. It is merely your ego's attempt to involve you in distractions that keep you from your real responsibility. Think again about your attraction to struggle. It is your attraction to the game, a game you hope to win, another chance to show your stamina and your strength, your quick wits and your cunning mind. It is another chance to prevail against the odds so stacked against you that you can once again convince yourself that you alone have succeeded against mighty adversaries. It is the only way you see to prove your power and control over a world of chaos. To not engage in the chaos at all is seen not as desirable, but as a sort of abdication, a loss through failure to engage. Although you are well aware you will not win the game you play here, you see the effort to do so, no matter how futile, as being that which makes up your life. To not engage is to not prove your own existence.

1.15   This is what you have made this world for: To prove your separate existence in a world apart from your creator. This world does not exist. And you do not exist apart from your creator. Your yearning for love is what tells you this is so. It is the proof you do not recognize.

What could cause you to yearn for love in a loveless world? 1.16
By what means do you continue to recognize that love is at
the heart of all things even while it is not valued here? Here
is a fine example that means and end are the same. For love
is what you are as well as what you strive for. Love is means
and end.

All the symbols of your physical life reflect a deeper mean- 1.17
ing that, while hidden to you, you still know exists. The
union of two bodies joined in love create a child, the union
of man and woman joined in marriage creates oneness.

Love is at the heart of all things. How you feel but reflects 1.18
your decision to accept love or to reject it and choose fear.
Both cannot be chosen. All feelings you label joyous or compassionate are of love. All feelings you label painful or angry
are of fear. This is all there is. This is the world you make.
Love or fear is your reality by your choice. A choice for love
creates love. A choice for fear creates fear. What choice do
you think has been made to create the world you call your
home? This world was created by your choice, and a new
world can be created by a new choice. But you must realize
that this is all there is. Love or lack of love. Love is all that is
real. A choice for love is a choice for heaven. A choice of fear
is hell. Neither is a place. They are a further reflection of
means and end being the same. They are but a further reflection of your power.

*I*nto this battlefield you have
bravely marched. The war rages by day and by night
and you have grown weary. Your heart cries out for
solace and does not go unheard. Help is here. — 2.20

What love is cannot be taught. It cannot be learned. But it   2.1
can be recognized. Can you pass love by and not know that
it is there? Oh, yes. You do it constantly by choosing to see
illusion rather than the truth. You cannot be taught love but
you can be taught to see love where it already exists. The
body's eyes are not the eyes with which love can be recognized. Christ's vision is. For only Christ's vision beholds the
face of God.

While you look for a God with a physical form you will not   2.2
recognize God. Everything real is of God. Nothing unreal
exists. Each person passing from this life to the next learns
no great secret. They simply realize love is all there is.
Nothing unreal exists. Think for yourself: If you were going
to die tomorrow what would you today find meaningful?
Only love. This is salvation's key.

Because love has no physical form you cannot believe that   2.3
love could be what you are, what you strive to be, what you
seek to return to. Thus you believe you are something other

than love and separate from love. You label love a feeling, and one of many. Yet you have been told there are but two from which you choose: love and fear. Because you have chosen fear so many times and labeled it so many things you no longer recognize it as fear. The same is true of love.

2.4   Love is the name you give to much you fear. You think that it is possible to choose it as a means to buy your safety and security. You thus have defined love as a reaction to fear. This is why you can understand love as fear's opposite. This is true enough. But because you have not properly recognized fear as nothing, you have not properly recognized love as everything. It is because of the attributes you have given fear that love has been given attributes. Only separate things have attributes and qualities that seem to complement or oppose. Love has no attributes, which is why it cannot be taught.

2.5   If love cannot be taught but only recognized, how is this recognition made possible? Through love's effects. For cause and effect are one. Creation is love's effect, as are you.

2.6   To believe that you are able to act in love in one instance and act in anger in another, and that both actions originate from the same place, is an error of enormous proportions. You again label love a "sometimes" component and think that to act in love more frequently is an achievement. You label acting from love "good" and acting out of anger "bad." You feel you are capable of loving acts of heroic proportions and fearful actions of horrific consequence, acts of bravery and acts of cowardice, acts of passion you call love and acts of passion you call violence. You feel unable to control the most extreme of these actions that arise from these extremes of feeling. Both "ends" of feelings are considered dangerous and a middle ground is sought. It is said that one can love too much and too little but never enough. Love is not something you do. It is what you are. To continue to identify love incorrectly is to continue to be unable to identify your Self.

To continue to identify love incorrectly is to continue to live   2.7
in hell. As much as highs and lows of intense feeling are sought by some to be avoided, it is in the in-between of passionless living that hell is solidified and becomes quite real. You can label joy heaven and pain hell and seek the middle ground for your reality thinking there are more than these two choices. A life of little joy and little pain is seen as a successful life, for a life of joy is seen as nothing more than a daydream, a life of pain a nightmare.

Into this confusion of love's reality you add the contents of   2.8
your history, the learned facts and the assumed theories of your existence. Although your purpose here remains obscure, you identify some things you call progress and others that you call evolution and you hope you have some miniscule role to play in advancing the status of humankind. This is the most you have any hope of doing, and few of you believe you will succeed. Others refuse to think of life in terms of purpose and thereby condemn themselves to purposeless lives, convinced one person among billions makes no difference and is of no consequence. Still others put on blinders to the world and seek only to make their corner of it more safe and secure. Some shift from one option to the next, giving up on one and hoping that the other will bring them some peace. To think that these are the only options available to creatures of a loving God is insane. Yet you believe that to think the opposite is true insanity. Given even your limited view of who you are, could this really be true?

The insanity of your thought processes and the world you   2.9
perceive must be made known to you before you are willing

to give them up. You do know this, and yet you constantly *forget*. This forgetting is the work of your ego. Your true Self does not want to forget, and cannot for even the tiniest fraction of a second. It is precisely the inability of your true Self to forget that gives you hope of learning to recognize love, and, with that recognition, of ending the insanity you now perceive.

2.10   Your real Self is the Christ in you. How could it be anything but love, or see with eyes other than those of love? Would you expect any decent human being to look on a loveless world, on misery and despair, and not be moved? Think not that those who seem to add to the world's misery are any exception. There is not a soul that walks this earth that does not weep at what it sees. Yet the Christ in you does not weep, for the Christ in you sees with eyes of love. The difference is the eyes of love see not the misery or despair. They are not there! This is the miracle. The miracle is true seeing. Think not that love can look on misery and see love there. Love looks not on misery at all.

2.11   Compassion is not what you have made of it. The Bible instructs you to be compassionate as God is compassionate. You have defined it unlike the compassion of God. To believe God looks upon misery and responds with sympathy and concern and does not end the misery is to believe in a God who is compassionate as you are compassionate. You think you would end misery if you could, beginning with your own, and yet you could no more end misery by making it real than could God. There is no magic here of turning misery into delight and pain into joy. These acts would indeed be magic, an illusion on top of an illusion. You have but accepted illusion as the truth, and so seek other illusions to change what never was into something that never will be.

To be compassionate as God is compassionate is to see as 2.12 God sees. Again, I stress to you, this is not about looking upon misery and saying to yourself you see it not. I am not an advocate of heartlessness but wholeheartedness. If you believe even the tiniest fraction of what is true, if you but believe you are a small part of God no bigger than a pinprick of light in a daunting sun, you still cannot believe in the reality of misery and despair. If you do, you believe this is the state of God as well. And if this were true, what hope would there be for misery's end? What light would there be in the universe that could end the darkness?

Reverse this thought and see if it makes any more sense than 2.13 it did before. In this scenario a benevolent and loving God who has extended His being into the creation of the universe has somehow managed to extend what is not of Him, to create what is unlike to His being in every way. Would even you attempt such folly? Would you conceive of the inconceivable?

What answer then is left but that you do not see reality for 2.14 what it is? What benefit is left to you in seeing incorrectly? What risk in attempting to see anew? What would a world without misery be but heaven?

Look not to figures from the past to show you the way 2.15 beyond illusions to the present. Look within to the one in you who knows the way. Christ is within you and you rest within God. I vowed to never leave you and to never leave you comfortless. The Holy Spirit has brought what comfort you would accept to your troubled mind. Now turn to me to comfort your troubled heart.

You have not sufficiently reversed your thinking, or your 2.16 heart would not still be troubled. The reversal has not occurred because you separate mind and heart and think you can involve one without involving the other. You believe that to know with your mind is a learning process that stands apart from all else that you are. Thus you can know without that knowing being who you are. You think you can love without love being who you are. Nothing stands apart from your being. Nothing stands alone. All your attempts to keep things separate are but a reenactment of the original separation made to convince yourself that the separation actually occurred.

2.17   You do not stand separate and alone. At these words your heart rejoices and your mind rebels. Your mind rebels because it is the stronghold of the ego. Your thought system is what has made the world you see, the ego its constant companion in its construction.

2.18   Yet your mind too rejoiced in the learning of all the teachings that have brought you here, congratulating itself on a feat that brought it rest. It is from this rest that the heart begins to be heard.

2.19   Just as the Holy Spirit can use what the ego has made, the ego can use what the mind has learned but has not integrated. Until you are what you have learned, you leave room for the ego's machinations. Once you are what you have learned, there is no room in which the ego can exist and, banished from the home you made for it, it slowly dies. Until this happens, the ego takes pride in what the mind has acquired, even unto the greater peace and contentment offered by your learning. It can and does see itself as better and stronger and more capable of worldly success. It would use all you have learned for its own motivations and pat you on the back for your new abilities. Without your vigilance it may even seem to have become stronger than before and fiercer in its criticism. It pretends to hold you to new standards, only to use what you have learned to increase your guilt. Thus it wins in daily battles and works for your final abdication, the day that you give up and admit defeat. It challenges your right to happiness and love and miracles, and seeks only to have you claim that living with such fantasies does not work and will not ever be possible here.

Into this battlefield you have bravely marched. The war rages by day and by night and you have grown weary. Your heart cries out for solace and does not go unheard. Help is here. 2.20

Do not believe that all that you have learned will not do what it was given you to do. Do not believe in your failure or the ego's success. All you have learned is still with you regardless of your perception of the outcome of your learning. Your perception of an outcome within your control is all that needs to change. Remember that cause and effect are one. What you want to learn you cannot fail to learn. 2.21

We will begin by working on a state of neutrality in which the war is no longer fought, the daily battles cease. Who wins and who loses is not of concern to us here. Peace has not yet come. But the white flag of surrender has been waved and dropped upon a hallowed ground where neutrality will for a short time reign before peace breaks out with glad rejoicing. 2.22

There are no plunders to be treasured. No victors of this war. All that has been learned and learned again is that this is what you do not want. Freedom to return home, away from cries of agony, defeat, and vainglory is all that now is sought. A state of neutrality is where the return begins. Armies may not yet be marching home, but their preparation is underway. 2.23

Such foolishness as the heart's desires will save you now. Remember it is your heart that yearns for home. Your heart that yearns for love remembered. Your heart that leads the way that, should you follow, will set you certainly on the path for home. — 3.18

Love is. It teaches by being what it is. It does not do any- 3.1 thing. It does not strive. It neither succeeds nor fails. It is neither alive nor dead. And thus it always was and always will be. It is not particular to you as human beings. It *is* in relationship to everything. All to all.

Just as true knowledge cannot be learned, love cannot be 3.2 learned and you cannot be learned. All that you desire and cannot learn is already accomplished. It is accomplished in you. It is you. Imagine the ocean or the cheetah, the sun or the moon or God Himself, attempting to learn what they are. They are the same as you. All exist within you. You are the universe itself.

It is a shared universe with no divisions. There are no sec- 3.3 tions, no parts, no inside and no outside, no dreams and no illusions that can escape or hide, disappear, or cease to be. There is no human condition that does not exist in all humans. It is completely impossible for one to have what another does not have. All is shared. This has always been true and is endlessly true. Truth is truth. There are no degrees of truth.

3.4 You are not form, nor is your real world. You seek the face of God in form as you seek for love in form. Both love and God are there, but they are not the form that your body's eyes see. Just as these words you see upon this page are symbols only of meaning far beyond what the symbols can suggest, so too is everything and everyone around you, those you see and those you only can imagine. To seek the "face" of God, even in the form of Christ, is to seek for what is forever without form. To truly see is to begin to see the formless. To begin to see the formless is to begin to understand what you are.

3.5 All that you now see are but symbols of what is really there before you, in glory beyond your deepest imaginings. Yet you persist in wanting only what your eyes can see and hands can hold. You call these things real and all else unreal. You can close your eyes and believe that you are in the dark, but you will not believe that you are no longer real. Close your eyes on all that you have become accustomed to seeing. And you will see the light.

3.6 In the light that comes only to eyes that no longer see, you will find the Christ who abides in you. In Jesus Christ, the Son of God became the son of man. He walked the world with a face much like your own, a body with two legs and two arms, ten fingers and ten toes. And yet you know this was not Jesus, nor is this a picture of the Christ. Jesus gave a face to love, as you do here as well. But love did not attach itself to form and say, "This is what I am." How can anything have a form except in symbols? A family crest, a mother's ring, a wedding band are all the same: They but represent what they symbolize in form.

There is no form that is not thus. A form is but a represen-   3.7
tation. You see a thousand forms a day with different names
and different functions and you think not that they are all
the same. You place values on each one based on usefulness
or pleasant appearance, on popularity or on reputation.
Each one you place in relationship to yourself, and so you
do not even see the form as it is but only as what it will do
for you. You imprison form within your meaning, and still
your meaning is truer than its form. You give all meaning to
everything, and thus you populate your world with angels
and with demons, their status determined by who would
help you and who would thwart you. Thus do you determine your friends and your enemies, and thus you have
friends who become enemies and enemies who become
friends. While a pencil may essentially remain a pencil in
your judgment, at least as long as it has all the qualities that
you have determined that a pencil should have, few people
can exhibit the qualities you have predetermined that they
should possess at all times and in all places. And so one dis-
appoints and another enthralls, one champions your cause
and another denigrates you. In all scenarios you remain the
maker of your world, giving it its causes and effects. If this
can be so, how can the world be anything but symbolic,
with each symbol's meaning chosen by you and for you.
Nothing is what it is, but only what it is to you.

Into this rank confusion is brought a simple statement: *Love*   3.8
is. Never changing, symbolizing only itself, how can it fail to
be everything or to contain all meaning? No form can
encompass it for it encompasses all form. Love is the light in
which form disappears and all that is, is seen as it is.

You who are looking for help wonder now how this would   3.9
help you. What is there left to say that has not been said?
What are these words but symbols, by my own admission? It

is in what they symbolize that help arrives. You do not need to believe in the words nor the potential of the exercises to change your life, for these words enter you as what they are, not the symbols that they represent. An idea of love is planted now, in a garden rich with what will make it grow.

3.10   Everything has birth in an idea, a thought, a conception. Everything that has been manifested in your world was first conceived within the mind. While you know this is true, you continue to believe you are the effect and not the cause. This is partially due to your concept of the mind. What you conceive it to be, it will be to you. While many teachings have attempted to dislodge this concept that you hold so dear, because you use the mind to deal in concepts, you have been unable to let new learning have its effect. This is because you believe your mind is in control of what it thinks. You believe in a process of input and output, all completely human and scientifically provable. The birth of an idea is thus the result of what has come before, of seeing something old as new, of improving on a former idea, of taking various information and collecting it into a new configuration.

3.11   What has this meant for learning that is not of this world? It means that you filter it through the same lens. You think of it in the same way. You seek to gather it together so that it will provide an improvement to what has been before. You look for evidence that shows that if you behave in a certain way certain things will happen as a result. Like a child learning not to touch a stove because it is hot and a burn will result, or learning that a warm blanket is comforting, you subject it to a thousand tests dependent on your senses and your judgment. While you believe you know what will hurt you and what you will find comforting, you subject what cannot be compared to the comparable.

Think not that your mind as you conceive of it learns with-   3.12
out comparison. Everything is true or false, right or wrong,
black or white, hot or cold, based solely on contrast. One
chemical reacts one way and one reacts another, and it is only
in the study of the two that you believe learning takes place.

You have not given up the idea that you are in control of   3.13
what you learn, nor have you accepted that you can learn in
a way that you have not learned before. Thus we move from
head to heart to take advantage of your concepts of the
heart, concepts much more in line with learning that is not
of this world.

These words of love do not enter your body through your   3.14
eyes and take up residence in your brain, there to be distilled
into a language that you can understand. As you read, be
aware of your heart, for this is where this learning enters and
will stay. Your heart is now your eyes and ears. Your mind
can remain within your concept of the brain, for we bypass
it now and send it no information for it to process, no data
for it to compute. The only change in thinking you are
asked to make is to realize that you do not need it.

What this will mean to you goes far beyond the learning of   3.15
this course. One such concept, given up and not replaced,
will free you beyond your deepest imaginings and free your
brothers and sisters as well. Once one such concept is felled,
others follow quickly. But none is more entrenched than this
one, the one we begin today to let fall away.

You who have been unable to separate mind from body,   3.16
brain from head, and intelligence from knowledge, take
heart. We give up trying. We simply learn in a new way and
in our learning realize that our light shines from within our
heart, our altar to the Lord. Here the Christ in us abides and

here we concentrate our energies and our learning, soon to learn that what we would know cannot be computed in the databanks of an overworked and over-trusted brain, a mind we cannot separate from where we believe it to be.

3.17   Our hearts, in contrast, go out to the world, to the suffer-ing, to the weak of body and of mind. Our hearts are not so easily contained within the casing of our flesh and bone. Our hearts take wing with joy and break with sadness. Not so the brain that keeps on registering it all, a silent observer, soon to tell you that the feelings of your heart were foolish-ness indeed. It is to our heart that we appeal for guidance, for there resides the one who truly guides.

3.18   You who think that this idea is rife with sentiment, sure to lead you to abandoning logic, and thereafter certainly to cause your ruin, I say to you again: take heart. Such foolish-ness as the heart's desires will save you now. Remember it is your heart that yearns for home. Your heart that yearns for love remembered. Your heart that leads the way that, should you follow, will set you certainly on the path for home.

3.19   What pain has your heart endured that it has failed to treas-ure for its source? Its source is love, and what greater proof need you of love's strength? Such pain as has your heart endured would surely be a knife to cut through tissue, a blow that to the brain would stop all functioning, an attack upon the cells far greater than any cancer. The pain of love, so treasured that it cannot be let go, can and does indeed attack the tissue, brain, and cells. And then you call it illness and allow the body to let you down, still and always holding love unto yourself.

3.20   Must pain accompany love and loss? Is this the price you pay, you ask, for opening up your heart? And yet, should you be asked if you would have other than the love you would not answer yes. What else is worth such cost, such suffering, so many tears? What else would you not let go when pain comes near, as a hand would drop a burning ember? What other pain would you hold closely, a grief not to be given up? What other pain would you be so unwilling to sacrifice?

Think not that these are senseless questions, made to bring   3.21
love and pain together and there to leave you unaided and unhelped, for pain and love kept together in this way makes no sense, and yet makes the greatest sense of all. These questions merely prove love's value. What else do you value more?

Your thoughts might lead you to a dozen answers now, more   3.22
for some and less for others, your answers depending on the tenacity of your thoughts, which, led by your ego, would throw logic in love's way. Some others might use their thoughts in yet another manner, claiming to choose love and not pain when what they really choose is safety at love's expense. No one here believes they can have one without the other and so they live in fear of love, all the while desiring it above all else.

Think you not that love can be kept apart from life in any   3.23
way. But we begin now to take life's judgment from it, the judgments gained by your experience, judgment based on how much love you have received and how much love has been withheld from you. We begin by simply accepting the proof we have been given of love's strength. For this we will return to again and again as we learn to recognize what love is.

All your long search for proof of God's existence ends here when you recognize what love is. And with this proof is proof of your existence established as well. For in your longing for love, you recognize as well your longing for your Self.

— 4.4

Do you have to love God to know what love is? When you love purely, you know God whether you realize it or not. What does it mean to love purely? It means to love for love's sake. To simply love. To have no false idols. 4.1

False idols must be brought to light and there seen as the nothing that they are before you can love for love's sake. What is a false idol? What you think love will get you. You are entitled to all that love would give but not to what you think love will provide for you through its acquisition. This is a classic example of not recognizing that "love is." 4.2

Love and longing are so intimately attached because they joined together at the moment of separation when a choice to go away from love and a choice to return were birthed in unison. Love was thus not ever lost but shadowed over by longing that, placed between you and your Source, both obscured Its light and alerted you of Its eternal presence. Longing is your proof of love's existence, for even here you would not long for what is not remembered. 4.3

4.4   All your long search for proof of God's existence ends here when you recognize what love is. And with this proof is proof of your existence established as well. For in your longing for love, you recognize as well your longing for your Self. Why would you wonder who you are and what your purpose here is all about, if not for your recognition, given witness by your longing, of what you fear you are not, but surely are?

4.5   All fear ends when proof of your existence is established. All fear is based on your inability to recognize love and thus who you are and who God is. How could you not have been fearful with doubt as powerful as this? How can you not rejoice when doubt is gone and love fills all the space that doubt once occupied? No shadows linger when doubt is gone. Nothing stands between the child of God and the child's own Source. There remain no clouds to block the sun, and night gives way to day.

4.6   Child of God, you are alien here but need not be alien to your Self. In your knowledge of your Self, all threat of time and space and place dissolves. You may still walk an alien land, but not in a fog of amnesia that obscures what would be a brief adventure and replaces it with dreams of terror and confusion so rampant that no toehold of security is possible, and day turns endlessly into night in a long march toward death. Recognize who you are and God's light goes before you, illuminating every path and shining away the fog of dreams from which you waken undisturbed.

4.7   Love alone has the power to turn this dream of death into a waking awareness of life eternal.

4.8   Yearning, learning, seeking, acquiring, the need to own, the need to keep, the grasping call, the driving force, the chosen passion — all these things that you have made to replace what you already have will lead you back as surely as they can lead you astray. Where what you have made will lead rests only on your decision. Your decision, couched in many forms, is simply this: to proceed toward love or to withdraw from it, to believe it is given or withheld.

Love is all that follows the law of God in your world. All else 4.9 assumes that what one has is denied another. While love cannot be learned nor practiced, there is a practice we must do in order to recognize love's presence. We practice living by the law of love, a law of gain not loss, a law that says the more you give the more you gain.

There are no losers and no winners under God's law. Not 4.10 one is given more than another. God cannot love you more than your neighbor, nor can you earn more of God's love than you have, or a better place in Heaven. The mind, under the ego's direction, has thrived on winners and on losers, on striving for and earning a better place. The heart knows not these distinctions, and those who think their hearts have learned them by being battered and abused by their experience here, rejoice in knowing that it is not so. This seeming illusion is believed in because your mind has made it so. Your thoughts have reviewed and reviewed again all the pain that love has brought. It dwells on those occasions when love has failed because it does not recognize that love cannot fail.

Your expectations and false perceptions of your brothers and 4.11 sisters are what have caused you to believe that love can fail, be lost, withdrawn, or turned to hate. Your false perception of your Father is what has caused all other perceptions to be false, including the one you hold of your own Self.

When you think of acting out of love, your thoughts of love 4.12 are based on sentiment and must be challenged. Love is not being nice when you are feeling surly. Love is not doing good deeds of charity and service. Love is not throwing logic to the wind and acting in foolish ways that pass as gaiety but cannot masquerade as joy. You each have an image in your mind of someone you believe knows what love is. This is perhaps an elderly person who is always kind and gentle, with no cross word for anyone, and no concern for his or her own self. This is perhaps a mother whose love is blind and self-sacrificing. Still others of you might imagine a couple long married in which each person is devoted to the other's happiness, or a father whose love is unconditional, or a priest or minister who guides unfailingly. For each or any one of these that you admire, you give attributes that you do not have and that you might one day acquire when the time is right. For that kind and gentle stance you do not believe will serve you now, that blindness and self-sacrifice is something to be gained at too high a price, that devotion you might think is fine for one whose partner is more loving than your own, that uncondi-tional love is great, but must it not be tempered by good judg-ment? And surely that ability to guide others must be earned through the acquisition of wisdom not within your reach.

4.13   Thus, your image of love is based upon comparison. You have chosen one who demonstrates that which in you is most lacking and you use that image to chastise yourself while saying this is what you want.

4.14   Your ideas of being in love are quite another category all together. In this context love is not only full of sentiment but of romance. This stage of love is seldom seen as lasting or as something that can be maintained. It is the purview of the young, and the daydream of the aging. It is synonymous with passion and an overflow of feelings that defy all com-mon sense. To be in love is to be vulnerable, for once common sense has failed to keep you acting as expected, you might forget to guard your heart or to keep your real Self in hiding. How dangerous indeed is such an act in a world where trust can turn to treachery.

Each one of you has held an ideal of what the perfect mate   4.15 would mean, an ideal that changed over time. Those most bound by the ego might think of stature and of wealth, of physical beauty and the trappings of good upbringing. Those most insecure will believe in a partner who would shower him or her with praise and gifts, with attention never wavering. Another who prizes independence seeks a partner in good health, not too demanding, a companion and a lover who will be convenient within a busy life.

You believe you can fall in love with the wrong person and   4.16 make a better choice based upon criteria more important than love. You thus believe love is a choice, something to be given to some and not to others. You hope to be a winner in this game you play, a chosen one who will have each ounce of love that is given returned in kind. This is a balancing act you play with God's most holy gift, resenting giving love that gains you little in return. And yet in this resentment you recognize the truth of what love is.

In no other area of life do you expect such fairness, such   4.17 exchange of equal value. You give your mind to an idea, your body to a job, your days to activities that do not interest or fulfill you. You accept what you are paid within certain boundaries you have set; you expect that a certain amount of prestige will follow certain accomplishments; you accept that some tasks have to be done for survival's sake. You hope there will be some fairness here in what you give and what you are given back. You hope your hard work will produce results, the dinner you prepared be eaten with delight, your ideas greeted as inspired. But this you do not expect. You often, in fact, expect the reverse to be the case, and are grateful for each acknowledgment the world gives you for the ways in which you spend your days. For spend your days you do, and soon that spending will deplete the limited number of days in store for you and you will die. Life is not fair, nor meant to be, you claim. But love is something else.

4.18   In this you are correct, for love is nothing like your image of your life and has no resemblance to how you spend your days or the way your days will end. Love is all that is set apart in your perception from what you do here. You think this setting apart gives love little relevance to other areas of your life. Love is seen as personal, something another gives in a special way to you alone, and you to him or her. Your love life has nothing to do with your work life, your issues of survival here, your ability to achieve success, or the state of your health and general welfare.

4.19   Even you who do not recognize what love is protect what you call love from the illusions you have made.

4.20   A thing set apart from the madness of the world is useful now. It may not be what love is, but what love is has guided you in choosing to set love apart from what you call the *real world*, from that which is, in fact, the sum total of what you have made. The world you struggle so to navigate is what you have made it, a place where love fits not and enters not in truth. But love has entered you and leaves you not, and so you too must have no place in this world that you have made but must have another where you are at home and can abide within love's presence.

4.21   The lucky ones among you have made a place resembling home within your world. It is where you keep love locked away behind closed doors. It is where you return after your forays into the world that you have made and upon entering believe you leave the world's madness outside your door. Here you feel safe and gather those you love around you. Here you share your day's adventures, making sense of what you can and leaving out the rest, and here you gain the strength you need to walk outside those doors again another day. You spend your life intent upon retiring to this safe place you have made of love in a world of madness, and hope that you will live to see the day when you can leave the madness behind, and that you will still find love behind the doors you have passed through so many times in a journey spent earning your right to leave it no more.

Some would call such a life selfish and wonder how the occupants of this semi-happy dream have earned the right to turn their backs upon the world even for the scanty hours that they make believe they can do so. Full-scale interaction with the world of madness is all that some are willing to accept of others or themselves. These are the angry ones who would demand that others bring what love they have into the madness to take responsibility for the mess that has been made, to attempt to restore order to chaos, anything so that the angry ones feel less alone with what their anger shows them. Love, they say, cannot be set apart, and so they feel love not, nor see it either. Yet they too recognize love for what it is when they scream, "You cannot have it while all of these do not. You cannot hoard it to yourself when so many are in need." 4.22

Everywhere you look is proof of love's difference found. This difference is your salvation. Love is not like anything or everything else that goes on here. And so your places to worship love have been built, your sacraments protect love's holiness, your homes host those you love most dearly. 4.23

4.24   Thus has your perception of love prepared you for what love is. For within you is the altar for your worship, within you has love's holiness been protected, within you abides the Host who loves all dearly. Within you is the light that will show you what love is and keep it not set apart from life any longer. Love cannot be brought to the world of madness, nor the world of madness brought to love. But love can allow a new world to be seen, a world that will allow you to abide within love's presence.

4.25   Take all the images of love set apart that you have made and extend them outside love's doors. What difference would a world of love make to those who lock their doors upon the world? How vast the reaches where their world of love could extend once love joined the world. How little need for the angry ones to retain their anger when love has joined the world. For love does join the world, and it is within this joining that love abides, holy as itself.

4.26   The world is but a reflection of your inner life, the reality unseen and unprepared for by all your strategy and defenses. You prepare for everything that goes on outside yourself and nothing that occurs within. Yet it is a joining that occurs within that brings about the joining of all the world for all the world to see. This joining of the world within is but your recognition of what love is, safe and secure within you and your brother, as you join together in truth. Think you not that this joining is a metaphor, a string of pleasant words that will bring you comfort if you heed them, one more sentiment in a world where lovely words replace what they would mean. This joining is the goal you seek, the only goal worthy of love's call.

4.27   This goal is set apart from all others as love is here, a goal that touches not on what you perceive to be a loveless world.

It has no relation to the world outside of you, but every relation to the world within, where in love's presence both outer and inner worlds become as one and leave beyond your vision the world that you have seen and called your home. This foreign world where you have been so lonely and afraid will linger for a while where it can terrify you no longer, until finally it will fade away into the nothingness from which it came as a new world rises up to take its place.

It is in every joining, every entering into, that love exists. Every joining, every entering into, is preceded by a suspension of judgment. Thus what is judged cannot be joined nor entered into where it can be understood. What is judged remains outside of you, and it is what remains outside that calls you to do what love would call you not to do. What remains outside is all that has not joined with you. What has joined with you becomes real in the joining, and what is real is only love. — 5.12

The Christ in you is wholly human and wholly divine. As 5.1 the wholly divine, nothing is unknown. As the wholly human, everything has been forgotten. Thus we begin to relearn the known as the One who already possesses all. It is this joining of the human and divine that ushers in love's presence, as all that caused you fear and pain falls away and you recognize again what love is. It is this joining of the human and divine that is your purpose here, the only purpose worthy of your thought.

You who have so filled your mind with senseless wanderings 5.2 and thoughts that think of nothing that is real, rejoice that there is a way to end this chaos. The world you see is chaos and nothing in it, including your thoughts, are trustworthy. This is why your thoughts must be newly dedicated, dedicated to the only purpose worthy of your thought: the purpose of joining with your real Self, the Christ in you.

I said earlier, it is only through union with me that you 5.3 learn, because it is only in union with me that you are your

Self. Now we must expand your understanding of union and of relationship as well as your understanding of me.

5.4 Union is impossible without God. God is union. Is this not like saying God is Love? Love is impossible without union. The same is true of relationship. God creates all relationship. When you think of relationship, you think of one relationship and then another. The one you share with this friend or that, with husband or wife, with child or employer or parent. In thinking in these specific terms you lost the meaning of the holy relationship. Relationship itself is holy.

5.5 Relationship exists apart from particulars. This is what you can't conceive of and what your heart must newly learn. All truth is generalizable because truth is not concerned with any of the specific details or forms of your world. You think relationship exists between one body and another, and while you think this is so, you will not understand relationship or union or come to recognize love as what it is.

5.6 Relationship is what exists between one thing and another. It is not one thing or another thing. It is not a third thing in terms of being a third object, but it is something separate, a third something. You realize that a relationship exists between your hand and a pencil when you go to write something down, but it is a relationship you take so completely for granted that you have forgotten that it exists. All truth lies in relationship, even one so simple as this. The pencil is not real, nor the hand that grasps it. Yet the relationship between the two is quite real. "When two or more are joined together" is not an injunction for bodies to unite. It is a statement that describes the truly real, the only reality that exists. It is the joining that is real and that causes all creation to sing a song of gladness. No one thing exists without another. Cause and effect are one. Thus, one thing cannot cause another without their being one or joined in truth.

We are beginning now to paint you a new picture, a picture 5.7 of things unseen before but visible to your heart if not your eyes. Your heart knows love without a vision of it. You give it form and say, "I love this one" or "I love that," yet you know that love exists apart from the object of your affection. Love is set apart in a frame not of this world. You hold objects up to capture it, to put a frame around love's vision and say, "This is it." Yet once you have it captured and hanging for all to look at and behold, you realize this is not love at all. You then begin your building of defenses, your evidence to cite to say, "Yes indeed, this is love and I have it here. It hangs upon my wall and I gaze upon it. It is mine to own and keep and cherish. As long as it is where I can look upon it, it is real to me and I am safe."

"Ah," you think when you find love, "now my heart is 5.8 singing; now I know what love is all about." And you attach the love you have found to the one in whom you found it and seek immediately to preserve it. There are millions of museums to love, far more than there are altars. Yet your museums cannot preserve love. You have become collectors rather than gatherers. Your fear has grown so mighty that all that would combat it is collected for safekeeping. Like the frame of love upon your wall, the collections that fill your shelves, whether they are of ideas or money or things to look at, are your desperate attempts to keep something for yourself away from all the rest. In setting love apart, you recognized it had no place here; but you went on to set yourself apart and all else that you could find to define as valuable. You build your banks as well as your museums as palaces to your love and no longer see the golden calves hiding within the palace walls.

5.9   This urge to preserve things is but your urge to leave a mark upon the world, a mark that says, "I have acquired much in my time here. These things I love are what I leave the world, what I pass down; they declare that I was here." Again you have the right idea, yet it is so sadly displaced as to make a mockery of who you are. Love does mark your place — but in eternity, not here. What you leave behind is never real.

5.10   Love gathered together is a celebration. Love collected is but a mockery of love. This difference must be recognized and understood, as must the urge to set love apart from all the rest, for with understanding these urges can be made to make sense. With understanding they can begin to bring sanity to an insane world.

5.11   You do not yet believe nor understand that the urges that you feel are real, and neither good nor bad. Your feelings in truth come from love, your response to them is what is guided by fear. Even feelings of destruction and violence come from love. You are not bad, and you have no feelings that can be labeled so. Yet you are misguided concerning what your feelings mean and how they would bring love to you and you to love.

5.12   It is in understanding the relationship that exists between what you feel and what you do that love's lessons are learned. Each feeling requires that you enter into a relationship with it, for it is there you will find love. It is in every joining, every entering into, that love exists. Every joining, every entering into, is preceded by a suspension of judgment. Thus what is judged cannot be joined nor entered into where it can be understood. What is judged remains outside of you, and it is what remains outside that calls you to do what love would call you not to do. What remains outside is all that has not joined with you.

What has joined with you becomes real in the joining, and what is real is only love.

Do you see the practicality of this lesson? What terror can be caused by an urge to violence that, once joined with love, becomes something else? An urge to violence may mean many things, but always lurking behind it is an overwhelming desire for peace. Peace may mean destruction of the old, and love can facilitate the rise and fall of many armies. What armies of destruction will rock the world when they are brought to love? 5.13

Within you is all the world safe, sure, and secure. No terror reigns. No nightmares rule the night. Let me give you once again the difference between what is within and what is without: Within is all that has joined with you. Without is all that you would keep separate. Within you is every relationship you have ever had with anything. Outside of you is all that you have kept apart, labeled, judged, and collected on your shelves. 5.14

This is all the two worlds are made up of. The one you see as real is the one you keep outside of yourself, making it possible to look upon it with your body's eyes. The one you do not see and do not believe in is the one you cannot look outward to see, but is the one that nonetheless is truly real. To look inward at the real world requires another kind of vision: the vision of your heart, the vision of love, the vision of the Christ in you. 5.15

You look outside the doors of your home and, whether you see suburban streets bathed in lamplight, streets that steam with garbage and crime, or cornfields growing, you say that is the real world. It is the world you go out into in order to earn your living, receive your education, find your mate. But 5.16

the home in which you stand, much like your inner world, is where you live the life that makes the most sense. It is where your values are formed, your decisions are made, your safety found. This comparison is not idly drawn. Your home is within and it is real, as real as the home you have made within the world seems to be. You can say the real world is somewhere outside yourself, as you picture the real world being beyond your doors, but saying this cannot make it so.

5.17   It is your continuing desire to have a relationship only with the world without that causes such a world to remain. This is because your definition of relationship is not one of joining. What you join with becomes real. As you take it into yourself you thereby make it real because you make it one with your real Self. This is reality. All you do not join with remains outside and is illusion, for what is not one with you does not exist.

5.18   You thus become a body moving through a world of illusion where nothing is real and nothing is happening in truth. This illusionary world is full of things you have told yourself and been instructed that you have to do, but that you do not want to do. The more your life consists of such things, the smaller your reality becomes. All that would join with you and become part of the real world of your creation remains beyond your reach.

5.19   There is nothing in your world that cannot be made holy through relationship with you, for you are holiness itself. You do not know this only because you fill your mind and leave your heart empty. Your heart becomes full only through relationship or union. A full heart can overshadow a full mind, leaving no room for senseless thoughts but only for what is truly real.

The first and only exercise for your mind within this course   5.20
has already been stated: Dedicate your thought to union.
When senseless thoughts fill your mind, when resentments
arise, when worry comes, repeat the thought that comes to
open your heart and clear your mind: "I dedicate all thought
to union." As often as you need to replace senseless
thoughts, think of this and say it to yourself not once but a
hundred times a day if needed. You do not need to worry
about what to replace your senseless thoughts with, as your
heart will intercede by fulfilling its longing for union as soon
as you have expressed your willingness to let it do so.

You do not yet understand the strength of your resistance to   5.21
the union that would turn hell into heaven, insanity to peace.
You do not yet understand your ability to choose that which
you make real in your creation of the world. The only meaning possible for free will is this: what you choose to join with
you, and what you choose to leave outside of yourself.

Your desire to be separate is the most insane desire of which   5.22
you have conceived. Over all your longing for union you
place this desire to be separate and alone. Your entire resistance to God is based on this. You think you have chosen to
be separate from God so that you can make it on your own,
and while you long to return to God and the heaven that is
your home, you do not want to admit that you cannot get
there on your own. You thus have made of life a test, believing that you can pass or fail through your own effort. Yet the
more you struggle to do so on your own, the more you realize the futility of your efforts, even though you do not want
to admit that your efforts are futile. You cling to effort as if
it is the way to God, not wanting to believe all effort is in
vain or that a simple solution exists. A simple solution
within your world, a solution that requires no exertion on
your part, is seen to be of little value. The individual, you

reason, is made through all this effort and struggle and without it would not be. In this you are correct, for as you make
of yourself an individual, you deny yourself your union with
all others.

5.23   All your efforts to be an individual are concentrated on the
life of your body. Your concentration on the life of your
body is meant to keep your body separate. "Overcoming" is
your catch phrase here as you struggle to overcome all the
adversity and obstacles that would keep you from having
what you think you want to have. This is your definition of
life, and while it remains it defines the life you see as real. It
presents you with a thousand choices to make, not once but
many times, until you believe that your power of choice is a
fantasy and that you are powerless indeed. You thus narrow
what you want and go after it with single-minded determination, believing the only choice within your control is what
to work hard to obtain. If you let all the world recede and
concentrate on this one choice, you reason that you are
bound to eventually succeed. This is the extent of your faith
in your own ability to maneuver this world that you have
made; and if you finally do succeed, your faith is seen as justified. The cost is not examined nor acknowledged, yet when
this faith is realized the cost becomes quite real. Rather than
feeling as if you have gained, feelings of loss will now be
what you fight to overcome. What have you done wrong,
you wonder. Why are you not satisfied with all you have
achieved?

5.24   This *getting what you want* that drives your life is proven time
and time again to not be what you want once you have
achieved it. Yet you think when this occurs that you have
simply chosen the wrong thing and so choose another and
another, not stopping to realize that you choose among illusions. You are so surprised that you have not found happiness

in what you seek! You continue living life as a test, driving yourself to follow one accomplishment with another, sure that the next one or the next will be the one to do the trick.

A trick this is indeed, for what has once failed to work will surely fail again. Stop now and give up what you think you want. 5.25

Stop now and realize your reaction to these words, the strength of your resistance. Give up what you want? This is surely what you have expected God to ask of you and what you have spent your lifetime guarding against. Why should you make this sacrifice? What then would your life be for? You want so little really. How can you be asked to give this up? 5.26

You do want little, and only when you realize this can you proceed to claiming everything that is yours. 5.27

For every joining, every union that you enter into, your real world is increased and what is left to terrify you decreased. This is the only loss that union generates, and it is a loss of what was merely illusion. As union begins to look more attractive to you, you are beginning to wonder how it comes about. There must be some secret you do not know. What is the difference, you ask, between setting a goal and achieving it and joining with something? 5.28

These do not have to be two separate things, but are made so by your choice, the choice to achieve what you will on your own. This is all the difference there is between union and separation. Separation is all you perceive on your own. Union is all that you invite me into and share with God. You cannot be alone nor without your Father, yet your invitation is necessary for your awareness of this presence. As I once was, you are both human and divine. What your human self 5.29

has forgotten, your real Self retains for you, waiting only for your welcome to make it known to you once more.

5.30   God is known to you within relationships, as this is all that is real here. God cannot be seen in illusion nor known to those who fear him. All fear is fear of relationships and thus fear of God. You can accept terror that reigns in another part of the world because you feel no relationship to it. It is only in relationship that anything becomes real. This you realize and so you strive to keep far from you all that in relationship with you would add to your discomfort and your pain. To think that any relationship can cause terror, discomfort, or pain is where you err in thinking of relationship.

5.31   You think that to come in contact with violence is to have a relationship with it. This is not so. If this were so, you would be joined to all you come in contact with and the world would be heaven indeed, as all you see became blessed by your holiness. That you move through your world without relating to it in any way is what causes your alienation from the heaven it can be.

5.32   Remember now one lovely day, for each of you has had at least one that was a shining light in a world of darkness. A day in which the sun shown on your world and you felt part of everything. Every tree and every flower welcomed you. Every drop of water seemed to refresh your soul, every breeze to carry you to heaven. Every smile seemed meant for you, and your feet hardly seemed to touch the soft ground on which you walked. This is what awaits you as you join with what you see. This awaits you as you place no judgment on the world, and in so doing join with everything and extend your holiness across a world of grief, causing it to become a world of joy.

$\mathcal{T}$he challenge now is in creation rather than accomplishment. With peace, accomplishment is achieved in the only place where it makes any sense to desire it. With your accomplishment comes the freedom and the challenge of creation. Creation becomes the new frontier, the occupation of those too young to rest, too interested in living still to welcome the peace of dying. Those who could not change the world one iota through their constant effort, in peace create the world anew. — 6.17

Joining rests on forgiveness. This you have heard before 6.1 without understanding what it is you would forgive. You must forgive reality for being what it is. Reality, the truly real, is relationship. You must forgive God for creating a world in which you cannot be alone. You must forgive God for creating a shared reality before you can understand it is the only one you would want to have. You have to forgive this reality for being different than you have always imagined it to be. You have to forgive yourself for not being able to make it on your own, because you have realized the impossibility of doing so. You have to forgive yourself for being what you are, a being who exists only in relationship. You have to forgive all others for being as you are. They too cannot be separate, no matter how hard they try. Forgive them. Forgive yourself. Forgive God. Then you will be ready to begin learning just how different it really is to live in the reality of relationship.

Your brother does not exist apart from you, nor you from 6.2 your brother. This is reality. Your mind is not contained within your body but is one with God and shared equally with all alike. This is reality. The heart that is the center of your being is the center of everything that exists. This is reality. None of these things make you less than what you have perceived yourself to be, but they do make it impossible for you to be separate. You can desire what is impossible until the end of your days but you cannot make it possible. Why not forgive the world for being other than what you have thought it to be and begin to learn what it really is? This is what the world is here for. And when you have learned what it would teach you, you will have need of it no more, and you will gently let it go and find heaven in its place.

6.3   This is all that the words and symbols and forms and structures of your world have come to teach you, stated as simply and directly as is possible. You are neither separate nor alone and never were and never can you be. All your illusions were created in order to obscure this fact of your existence because you would rather it not be so. Only when you quit wishing for what cannot be, can you begin to see what is.

6.4   I was least accepted as prophet and savior by those who were most like me, those who watched me grow, worked alongside my parents, and lived in the same town. This was because they knew I was not different from them, and they could not accept that they were the same as me. They were then, and you are now, no different than I. We are all the same because we are not separate. God created the universe as an interrelated whole. That the universe is an interrelated whole is no longer disputed even by science. What you have made to hide your reality has been, with the help of the Holy Spirit, turned into that which will help you learn what your reality really is. Yet you still refuse to listen and to learn. You still prefer things to be other than what they are and, through your preference, choose to keep it so.

Make a new choice! The choice that your heart yearns to   6.5
make for you and that your mind is finding increasingly difficult to deny. When you choose unity over separation, you
choose reality over illusion. You end opposition by choosing
harmony. You end conflict by choosing peace.

All this forgiveness can do for you. Forgiveness of the origi-   6.6
nal error — the choice to believe that you are separate despite
the fact that this is not so and cannot ever be. What loving
creator would create a universe in which such a thing could
be? A thing alone would be a thing created without love, for
love creates like itself and is forever one with everything that
has been created. This simple realization will start you on the
path to learning what your heart would have you learn.

The fact that you are not alone in the world shows you that   6.7
you are not meant to be alone. Everything here is to help
you learn to perceive correctly, and from there to go beyond
perception to the truth.

What is the opposite of separation but being joined in rela-   6.8
tionship? Everything joined with you in relationship is holy
because of what you are. Every contrast that you see here but
points to this truth. Evil is only seen in relation to good.
Chaos is only seen in relation to peace. While you see these
as separate things you do not see what the relationship
would show you. Contrast demonstrates, which is why it is
a favorite teaching device of the Holy Spirit. Contrast
demonstrates only to reveal the relationship that exists
between truth and illusion. When you chose to deny relationship, you chose a thought system based on the opposite
of your reality. Thus each choice to deny union reveals its
opposite. What is separate from peace is chaos. What is separate from good is evil. What is separate from the truth is
insane. Since you cannot be separate, all these factors that

oppose your reality exist only in opposition to it. This is what you chose to create when you chose to pretend you can be what you cannot be. You chose to live in opposition to the truth, and the opposition is of your making.

6.9 Choose again! And let go your fear of what the truth will bring. What could be more insane than that which you now call sanity? What loss can there be in joining with what is so like yourself? It is only a small step away from where you currently stand, so helpless and alone.

6.10 Yet fear you do, and the maintenance of your fear keeps you very busy. You stoke its fire lest it go out and leave you to a warmth not of this world. This is the warmth that you would have, warmth so all pervasive no chill of winter need ever arise again. And yet, still you choose the fire. You choose the fires of hell to the light of heaven. Only you can stoke those fires, and this is what makes them desirable to you. A warmth not of this world, given freely, with no work involved, causes you to shake your head. How can it be for you if you cannot put in effort to attain it? And even if it were so, what then? Some, you think, might choose to live near the equator, to have the sun shine every day and the need to stoke the fire put behind them. But not you. You, you think, prefer the seasons, the cold as well as the warmth, the snow as well as the rain, the dark of night and the clouds that block the sun. Without all of these, what would life be? Perpetual sunshine would be too easy, too lacking in imagination, too sterile. To have every day the same would be uninteresting now. Perhaps later. Maybe when you are old and have grown weary of the world. Then perhaps you will sit in the sun.

6.11 This is the heaven of your mind, the meaning you give to joining, the face you put on eternal peace. With such a vision in your mind it is no wonder that you choose it not, or that you put it off until the end of your days. A heaven such as this would be for the old and the infirm, the ones ready to leave the world, those who have already grown worn out from it. What fun would such a heaven be for those of you still young and full of vigor? Those still willing to face another battle? Those who have not yet faced every challenge? If there is a mountain left to climb, why choose heaven? Surely it can be chosen later when disease has taken your limbs' use from your control and your mind no longer races forward to what is next.

Eagerness for life and eagerness for heaven are seen to be in opposition. Heaven and its milieu of eternal peace is rightly kept, you think, for the end of life, and so you scream at the unfairness when a young one leaves the world. Heaven is not for the young, you say. How unfair that those who die young have not had a chance at life, a chance to face the struggle and the challenge, the coming of the new day and the dying of the old. How sad they have not had the opportunity to stand separate and alone and to become what they would become. What they are is no more valued than what you are. What is still to come is what you live for, with the undying hope that it will not be that which came before. For every challenge faced is but a call to face the next. And each one comes to replace the old with hope that this one will be the one — and equal hope that it will not. 6.12

To succeed is but a little death from which you must hurry on to where the challenge of a new success and new reason to exist awaits. The carrot of fulfillment you hold before yourself when grasped is quickly eaten and life feeds on itself once again. Just as you eat to still your hunger only to become hungry again, so does the rest of your life need this constant maintenance to retain the 6.13

reality you have given it. "Struggle to succeed and succeed to struggle yet another day" is the life you have made, and the life you fear heaven would replace. To give up the idea that this is where meaning is found, fulfillment attained, happiness birthed amongst sorrow, is seen as giving up. Heaven's help is most called upon for just this time, this time when giving up is close, for never do you feel more in need of help than when all your plans have failed and giving up becomes an alternative more attractive than carrying on.

6.14 Few ask for the grace to give up what has been for what could be. For giving up is seen as failure, and here is what you fear the most. To not succeed at life would indeed be a failure if it were possible for it to be so. Yet even this possibility you would cling to, for with no chance of failure is no chance of success, or so you reason. The contrast that you have come to see in your separated state makes only either/or situations possible. While a choice for heaven is indeed a choice to renounce hell, while truth is indeed a choice to renounce illusion, these are the only real choices that exist, and they do not extend into your illusions but only into truth. For in truth are all illusions gone, in heaven is all thought of hell forever vanquished.

6.15 How can I convince you that peace is what you want when you do not know what peace is? Those who once worshiped golden calves did so because they knew of no other choice. A god of love was as foreign a concept to them as is a life of peace to you. What is foreign to the world has changed, but the world has not. Those who live with war seek peace. Those who live with failure seek success. Put another way, both are saying this: you seek to make sense of an insane world, to find meaning within meaninglessness, purpose among the purposeless.

How can I make peace attractive to you who know it not? 6.16
The Bible says, "The sun shines and the rain falls on the
good and evil alike." Why then do you think that peace is
endless sunshine? Peace is merely enjoyment of the rain and
sun, night as well as day. Without judgment cast upon it,
peace shines on all that you would look upon, as well as
every situation you would face.

Situations too are relationships. When peace enters your 6.17
relationships, situations, too, are what they are meant to be
and seen in heaven's holy light. No longer do situations pit
one against another, making it impossible for anyone to
achieve what they would achieve. The challenge now is in
creation rather than accomplishment. With peace, accomplishment is achieved in the only place where it makes any
sense to desire it. With your accomplishment comes the
freedom and the challenge of creation. Creation becomes
the new frontier, the occupation of those too young to rest,
too interested in living still to welcome the peace of dying.
Those who could not change the world one iota through
their constant effort, in peace create the world anew.

Here they find the loveliest of answers to their questions. It 6.18
takes not time nor money nor the sweat of their brow to
change the world: it takes only love. A forgiven world is
whole, and in its wholeness one with you. It is here, in
wholeness, that peace abides and heaven is. It is from wholeness that heaven waits for you.

Think about this now — for how could heaven be a sepa- 6.19
rate place? A piece of geography distinct from all the rest?
How could it not encompass everything and still be what it
is: home to God's beloved son and dwelling place of God
Himself? It is because God is not separate from anything
that you cannot be. It is because God is not separate from

anything that heaven is where you are. It is because God is love that all your relationships are holy, and from them you can find the way to Him and to your holy Self.

6.20   Are your relationships with those you love severed when they leave this world? Do you not still think of them? And do you not still think of them as who they were in life? What is the difference, in your mind, between who they were and who they are after death? In honesty you will admit an envy, an awareness that they still exist, but without the pain and burden of the body, without the limits placed upon those who remain. You imagine them still in bodily form, perhaps, yet you imagine them happy and at peace. Even those who claim not to believe in God or an afterlife of any sort will, when prompted to be truthful, admit this is an image that lights their mind with peace and hope. This image is as ancient as the earth and sky and all that lies beyond it. It did not arise from fantasy, nor did it pass from one mind to the next as stories often will. It is but part of your awareness of who you are, an awareness you would deny in favor of thoughts of death so grim they make of life a nightmare.

6.21   It is your denial of all your happy thoughts that has led you to a life of such unhappiness. Thoughts of terror and of sin you will embrace, but thoughts of resurrection and new life you still before they have a chance at birth and call them wishful thinking. What harm do you expect happy thoughts to do to you? At best you see them as delusional. But what you fear is disappointment. All that you have wished for and have not acquired within your life is the evidence you would use to deny yourself hope of any kind. You do not understand the difference between wishing for what can never be and accepting what is.

The world cannot fail to disappoint you, for your concep-   6.22
tion of it is based upon deception. You have deceived only
yourself, and your deception has not changed what is nor
will it ever succeed in doing so. Only God and His
appointed helpers can lead you from this self-deception to
the truth. You have been so successful at deception that you
no longer can see the light unaided. But join your brother
and the light begins to shine, for all are here to aid you. This
is the purpose of the world and of love most kind: to end
your self-deception and return you to the light.

What you would withhold from the world you withhold from yourself, for you are not separate from the world. In every situation what you would keep is what you will not have, because you keep it only from yourself. — 7.16

A major thought reversal is required now before we can go on. It has been stated and emphasized countless times before, and it will be here as well: What you give you will receive in truth. What you do not receive is a measure of what you withhold. Your heart is accustomed to giving in a way that your mind is not. Your mind would hold on to every idea for what it might bring you, and is resentful of those whose ideas do come to fruition and succeed in getting desirable things within this world. "I had that idea," you lament when another succeeds where you have failed. "I could have been where that person is if not for the unfairness of life," you wail. Your mind dwells in a world of its own made up largely of *if onlys*. Your heart, on the other hand, knows of giving and of a return not based on the world of your mind or of physical circumstance. Despite disappointments most severe, your heart knows that what you give you receive in truth. 7.1

And yet you would withhold a piece of yourself even from love, and this is what we must correct. For what you withhold 7.2

you cannot receive, and you cannot receive a piece of heaven nor know a piece of God or your own Self. Your giving must be total for you to receive in truth. We will concentrate more now, however, on withholding than on giving, for you do not yet understand what you would give, for you do not recognize what you *have* to give. You do, however, recognize what you withhold and can begin to recognize this in every situation. As the awareness of your withholding dawns upon your heart, you will begin to realize what you do not give, and with that realization, what you have to give.

7.3   Comparison of one thing to another — a comparison that seeks out differences and magnifies them and names one thing this and one thing that — is the basis of all learning in your world. It is based on contrast and opposites and on separating into groups and species. Not only is each individual distinct and separate, but so too are groups of individuals, pieces of land, systems and organizations, the natural world and the mechanistic world, heaven and earth, divine and human.

7.4   In order to identify yourself in this world, you have had to withhold a piece of yourself and say of this piece, "This is what makes me uniquely who I am." Without this piece of yourself that you have determined to be unique, your existence would seem to serve even less purpose than it does now. Thus that which is most separate, or that which you have determined separates you the most, is that which you value most highly.

7.5   This one thought constitutes a thought system in and of itself, for it is the primary thought by which you live your life. Your effort goes into maintaining this illusion that what you are must be protected, and that your protection rests on holding this piece of yourself separate. Like the love you set aside from this world, this thought too is one that can be used, for it recognizes that you are as apart from this world as love is. The harsh realities of the world may claim your body and your time, but this one piece of yourself that you have set aside you allow it not to claim. This piece is held within your heart, and it is this piece with which we now will work.

This is the piece that screams *never* to that which would beat you down. Life is seen as a constant taking away and this, you claim, will *never* be taken from you. For those whose lives are threatened, it is called the will to live. For those whose identity is threatened, it is called the cry of the individual. For others it is the call to create, and for still others the call to love. Some will not give up hope to cynicism. Others label it ethics, morals, values, and say this is the line I will *never* cross. It is the cry that says, "I will not sell my soul." 7.6

Rejoice that there is something in this world that you will not bargain with, something you hold sacrosanct. This is your Self. Yet this Self that you hold so dear that you will never let it go is precisely what you must be willing to freely give away. This is the only Self that holds the light of who you are in truth, the Self that is joined with the Christ in you. 7.7

To this Self is this appeal put forth. Let it be heard and held within your heart. Hold it joyously alongside what already occupies your heart — the love you set aside and the piece of yourself that you won't let go. As you learn that what you give you will receive in truth, you will see that what abides within your heart is all that is worthy of your giving and all you would receive. 7.8

Let us return now to what you would withhold, and see the effects that this withholding has upon your self and the 7.9

world that seems to hold you separate. This is, indeed, the first and most general lesson in regard to withholding: The world does not keep you separate. You keep yourself separate from the world. This is what has made the world the world it is. What you withhold allows illusion to rule and truth to be locked away in a vault so impenetrable and so long secured that you have thought it forgotten. You have not realized the vault is your own heart, or that the truth is what you have chosen to keep secure and set aside there. When you believe that this is so and that what you give away you will receive in truth, you will throw open the doors to this safe house, and all the joy you have kept from yourself will return. A great exchange will happen as a powerful wind sweeps through your heart, and all the love you have denied the world will be released. It will flow in every direction, leaving not a corner of the universe untouched. In an instant the eternal will be upon you. Death will be a dream as the wind of life reunited with itself gathers from directions that are beyond direction and breathes life back into what has so long been locked away. After this a gentle breeze will come, never again to leave you, as life breathes as one.

7.10   Your withholding takes on many forms that nonetheless are merely effects of the selfsame cause that keeps truth separate from illusion. Where truth has come illusion is no more. Truth has no need of your protection, for truth brought to illusion shines its light into the darkness, causing it to be no more.

7.11   There are but two forms of withholding: what you withhold *of* yourself from the world and what you withhold *for* yourself from the world. A grievance is something you have chosen for yourself, a piece of a relationship separated off and held in contempt and righteousness. You are unaware that you choose this form of withholding, sometimes dozens or even hundreds of times a day. An unreturned phone call, a bit of traffic, a harsh word spoken, an unremembered errand — all can be resentments you hold to yourself and refuse to let go. By the time you begin your day you may hold several of these in your mind, and there you build them into reasons for even further withholding. Now you have an excuse — or several excuses — for a *bad day*. Why should you give anything to anyone when your day has already treated you so badly? You withhold even a smile, because you have chosen grievances over love.

You might choose to tell those you encounter of your bad day, and if they are properly sympathetic you may feel that you have gotten something in exchange for the resentments you carry, and if the exchange is determined to be of equal value you might let them go. A response of less than sympathetic proportions, however, is simply added to your list of grievances until the burden of what you hang on to becomes more than you can bear. Now you look for one upon whom you can unload your burdens, hoping you can pass your grievances en masse to someone else. If you succeed through anger, spite, or meanness, you simply take on guilt and withdraw still further into your own misery. 7.12

What you do not realize is that every situation is a relationship — even those as simple as unreturned phone calls and snarled traffic. You relate to someone or something in every situation you encounter, and what you hold against them you withhold from them. You have taken a piece of them and hold it unkindly to yourself, not in joining but in separation. Totally unaware, you too are subject to these whims of your brothers and sisters, and find at times pieces of yourself scattered hither and yon, knowing they are lost to you but not knowing how this loss came about or where to retrieve these missing pieces, not knowing that you can 7.13

prevent the loss entirely by being one. What is joined can not be parceled out and scattered, but must remain in wholeness. What is joined resides in peace and knows no grievance. What is joined resides in love inviolate.

7.14   There is another way in which you withhold pieces of relationships for yourself. This withholding is not of the form of grievances but of the form of specialness. You withhold in order to make yourself special, always at another's expense. All your efforts to *best* your brothers and sisters are thus: all competition, all envy, all greed. These all relate to your image of yourself and your efforts to reinforce it. This is your desire not to be intelligent, but to be *more* intelligent than your colleague. This is your desire not to be generous, but to be *more* generous than your relative. This is your desire for wealth that is *greater* than your neighbors, attractiveness *greater* than that of your friends, success *greater* than that of the average man or woman. You pit yourself not only against individuals but groups and nations, teams and organizations, religions and neighbors and family members. This is the desire to be right, or in control, or to have more or be more. This is life based on comparison of illusion to illusion.

7.15   You do not see this as withholding, but what you claim for yourself at another's expense is indeed withholding, and in your world you know not how to claim anything for yourself without withholding it from someone else. You have now set yourself up in a position to withhold your intelligence from others lest they profit from it. You want your intelligence known and recognized, but you want it known and recognized as *yours*. If someone wants the intelligence you have to offer, something must be given in return. What you demand can range from admiration to money, but it is all the same and the demand is always there. It is the ransom that you insist be paid, the homage you claim is due, that without which you will withhold what you have. And you are thankful for these things with which you can demand ransom of the world, for without them you would be the one called upon to pay.

These are examples of what you withhold from the world *for* yourself. But what of that which you withhold from the world *of* yourself? Both these things are much the same in truth, for what you hold away from all the rest, what you hold for ransom and do not freely give, you do not have the use of for yourself. Those ideas that you save up, that creativity that only you would benefit from, that wealth you would amass —these things are as useless to you when saved for yourself alone as they would be if they did not exist. They bring you not to truth or happiness, nor can they buy you love or the success you seek. What you withhold from the world you withhold from yourself, for you are not separate from the world. In every situation what you would keep is what you will not have, because you keep it only from yourself. 7.16

We must return now to relationship and correct as quickly as possible any erroneous ideas you have, especially those that might make of this a trivial point or one that is specific and not generalizable. All relationship exists in wholeness. The small examples used earlier were meant to help you recognize relationship itself, relationship as something different from the objects, persons, or situations related to. Now we must expand on this idea. 7.17

Broadening your view from the specific to the general is one of the most difficult tasks of the curriculum. It is easy to see why this is so when you recognize how bound your thinking is to specifics. Again this is why we call on love and the 7.18

hidden knowledge of your heart. Your heart already sees in a manner much more whole than the perception of your split mind. Even your language and images reflect this truth, this difference between the wisdom of your heart and that of your mind. Your heart may be said to break, but the image that these words call forth is of a heart cracked open, not of a heart in separate pieces. Your brain, on the other hand, is separated into right and left hemispheres. One side has one function, one side another. While your brain and your mind are not the same, your image of your mind and what it does and does not do is linked with your image of your brain. Let this image go and concentrate on the wholeness of your heart, no matter how you view its current condition. Be it wounded, bleeding, broken, or full, it rests in wholeness within you at the center of who you are.

7.19   It is from this center that truth will light your way.

7.20   It is from this center that you will come to understand that relationship exists in wholeness. We have begun to dislodge your idea that you stand separate and alone, a being broken off from all the rest. Your forgiveness of all that has led to this misperception is not yet complete, nor will it be until your understanding is greater than it is now. For you cannot give up the only reality you know without believing in and having at least some elementary understanding of what the truth of your reality actually is.

7.21   If you cannot be alone you must be continuously in relationship. Thus, relationship must not depend on interaction as you understand it. It is easy to see the relationship between a pencil and your hand, your body and another, the actions that you do and the effects they seem to cause. All of these relationships are based on what your senses tell you, the evidence you have relied upon to make sense of your

world. Those who have developed reliance on ways of knowing not governed by the acceptable senses are seen as suspect.
And yet you accept many causes for your feelings, from varia-
tions in the weather to unseen and unverifiable diseases. You
have given others, who you see as having more authority
than you, license to provide you with their version of the
truth, and for consistency's sake you choose to believe in
the version of the truth most predominate in your society.
Thus the *truth* is different in one place than it is in another
and it even appears to be in conflict. You cling to known
truths, even though you are aware of their instability in time
as well as place, and so you live with constant denial that
even what is known to you is not known at all. You thus
cling to the one sure thing that permeates your existence:
the knowledge that death will claim you and all of those
you love.

Realize that when you are asked to give this up, you are   7.22
asked to give up an existence so morbid that anyone with
any sanity would gladly toss it to the wind and ask for an
alternative. An alternative exists. Not in dreams of fantasy
but in truth. Not in changing form and circumstance but in
eternal consistency.

Accept a new authority, even if only for the little while that   7.23
it will take you to read these words. Start with this idea: You
will allow for the possibility of a new truth to be revealed to
your waiting heart. Hold in your heart the idea that as you
read these words — and when you finish reading these
words — their truth will be revealed to you. Let your heart
be open to a new kind of evidence of what constitutes the
truth. Think of no other outcomes than your happiness, and
when happiness comes deny it not, nor its source. Remind
yourself that when love comes to fill your heart, you will
deny it not, nor its source. You do not need to believe that

this will happen, but only to allow for the possibility of it happening. Do not turn your back on the hope offered here, and when new life flows in to release the old, forget not from where it came.

CHAPTER 8 | the SEPARATION from
the BODY

*Safe within your heart lies
love's reality, a reality so foreign to you that you think
you remember it not. Yet it is to this reality we head as
we travel deep within you to the center of your Self.*
— 8.9

The thoughts of your heart you have defined as your emo- 8.1
tions. These thoughts stand apart from the wisdom of your
heart that we have already discussed — the wisdom that
knows to set love apart, as well as your own self. Emotions,
the thoughts of your heart, are what we will now work with,
separating as we do the truth from your perception of it.

This curriculum aims to help you see that your emotions are 8.2
not the real thoughts of your heart. What other language
might your heart speak? It is a language spoken so quietly
and with such gentleness that those who cannot come to
stillness know it not. The language of your heart is the language of communion.

Communion is union that we will speak of here as being of 8.3
the highest level, though in truth, no levels separate union
at all. As a learning being, the idea of levels is helpful to you
and will aid you in seeing that you progress from one step,
or one level of learning, to another. This is more a process of
remembering than learning, and this you will understand as

memory begins to return to you. Your heart will aid you in replacing thinking with remembering. In this way, remembering can be experienced as the language of the heart.

8.4 This remembering is not of former days spent upon this earth, but of remembering who you really are. It comes forth from the deepest part of you, from the center in which you are joined with Christ. It speaks of no experiences here, wears no faces, and bears no symbols. It is a memory of wholeness, of all to all.

8.5 Many emotions as well as thoughts would seem to block your way to the stillness in which this memory can be found. Yet as you have seen again and yet again, the Holy Spirit can use what you made for a higher purpose when your purpose is in union with that of spirit. We will thus examine a new way of looking at emotions, a way that will allow them to assist you in your learning rather than block you from it.

8.6 You think of the heart as the place of feeling, and thus you associate emotions with your heart. Emotions, however, are really reactions of your body to stimuli that arrive through your senses. Thus, the sight of a lovely sunset can bring tears to your eyes. The slightest contact between your hand and the skin of a baby can cause you to feel as if your heart overflows with love. Harsh words that enter through your ears can cause your face to redden and your heart to beat with a heaviness you label anger or a sting you would call shame. Problems that mount up and seem too much to bear can cause what you call emotional turmoil or even a nervous breakdown. In these situations either too many feelings are going on all at once or all feeling is shut down all at once. As with everything else in this world, you strive for a balance that allows your heart to beat at one steady pace, for one emotion to surface at a time, for feelings that you can control. And yet you feel controlled by your feelings, emotions that seem to have a life of their own, and a body that reacts to all of it in ways that make you uncomfortable, anxious, ecstatic, or terrified.

None of this speaks of what your heart would say to you, but   8.7
it masks the language of the heart and buries stillness deep beneath an ever-changing milieu of life lived on the surface, as if your own skin were the playground for all the angels and demons that would dance there. What you would remember is replaced by memories of these emotions — so many that they could not be counted even for one day, even by those who claim to have them not. It is not your thoughts to which you turn to bring you evidence for your resentment, ammunition for your vengeance, pain for your remembering. It is to your emotions, those feelings that you would say come from your own heart.

What foolishness to think love could abide with compan-   8.8
ions such as these. If these be in your heart, where is love? If these illusions were real there would be no place for love at all, but love abides where illusion cannot enter. These illusions are like barnacles upon your heart, adhering to its surface, but keeping it not from fulfilling its function or carrying within itself that which keeps you safe upon this raging sea.

Safe within your heart lies love's reality, a reality so foreign   8.9
to you that you think you remember it not. Yet it is to this reality we head as we travel deep within you to the center of your Self.

Even those of you whose perceptions remain quite faulty   8.10
know that there is a difference between what lies on the

surface and what lies beneath. Often the surface of a situation is all that is seen, the surface of a problem all that is recognized, the surface of a relationship all that is known to you. You speak openly of these levels of seeing, recognizing, and knowing, saying often, "On the surface it would seem that..." and this observation is often followed by attempts to see beneath the surface to find causes, motivations, or reasons for a situation, problem, or relationship. Often this search is called seeking for the truth. While the way in which you go about seeking for the truth in places it is not causes it to remain hidden from you, your recognition that a truth is available in a place other than on the surface is useful to us now, as is your recognition that something other than what appears *on the surface* exists.

8.11   What do you mean to do when you attempt to look beneath the surface? Do you mean to look beneath the skin, or into the hidden recesses of a heart or mind? Without union all your seeking will not reveal the truth. And while there is a part of you that knows this, you prefer instead of union a game of speculation, conjecture, and probable cause. You look for explanations and information rather than the truth you claim to seek. You look in judgment rather than in forgiveness. You look from separation's stance rather than from the grace-filled place of union. Perhaps you are thinking now that if you knew how this union worked you would surely use it to find the truth, and for other objectives as well. You would like to be a problem solver, a person who could, as in a court of law, separate right from wrong, truth from lies, fact from fiction. You do not even see that what you desire is further separation, and that separation cannot bring about the truth nor arise from unity.

8.12   Even your loftiest desires are fraught with righteousness that is still righteousness no matter what the noble cause you deem yourself willing to address. You would see into another's mind and heart in order perhaps to help them, but also to have power over them. Whatever you might come to know you would deem your property and its disposition your purview. How dangerous would you be if union were such as this? How rightly you would fight it to protect your own secrets from revelation. This faulty perception of union would keep you from the goal you seek, the goal that is no goal but your only reality, the natural state in which you would exist but for your decision to reject your reality and your true nature.

Do you see now why unity and wholeness go hand in hand? Why you cannot withhold a piece of yourself and realize the unity that is your home? Were it possible to exist in unity and still withhold, unity would be a mockery. Who would you withhold for? And who would you withhold from? Unity is wholeness. All for all. 8.13

We have talked now of what is on the surface. Let us try an experiment. Think of your body now as the surface of your existence and look upon it. Stand back from it, for it is not your home. The heart we speak of does not abide in it and nor do you. Separate bodies cannot unite in wholeness. They were made to keep wholeness from you and to convince you of the illusion of your separateness. Step back. See your body as just the surface layer of your existence. It is what appears to be and no more. Let it not keep you from seeing the truth, as you do not let other surface conditions hide the truth from you. Even if you have not formerly found the truth, you have recognized what is not the truth. Your body is not the truth of who you are, no matter how much it appears to be. For now, let's consider it the surface aspect of your existence. 8.14

8.15   We will go one step further as well, for many of you are thinking still that it is what is within the body that is real: your brain and heart, your thoughts and emotions. If your body contained what was real, it too would be real. Just as if a surface situation contained the truth, it would be the truth. If your body and what lies within it are not who you are, you feel as if you are left homeless. This feeling of homelessness is necessary for your return to your real home, for were you locked up and contained within your body, and were you to accept this container as your home, you would not accept another.

8.16   Your "other" home is the home you feel as if you have left and the home you feel the desire to return to. Yet it is where you are, and you could not be anywhere else. Your home is here. You think this is incongruous with the truth as I'm revealing it, the truth that heaven is your home, but it is not. There is no *here* in the terms that you would think of it, the terms that set your reality in a location, on a planet, in a body. *God is here* and you belong to God. This is the only sense in which you can or should accept the notion that you belong here. When you realize God is here, then and only then can you truthfully say *here* is where I belong.

8.17   Now that you are standing back from your body, participating in this experiment to recognize the surface element of your existence, you are perhaps more aware than ever before of being in a particular place and time. As you stand back and observe your body, this is what you will see: a form moving through time and place. You may be more aware than ever of its actions and complaints, its sturdiness or lack thereof. You may be realizing how it governs your existence and wondering how you could spend even a moment without awareness of it.

This moment without awareness of the body was beautifully   8.18
described in *A Course in Miracles* as the Holy Instant. You
may not think observation of your body is a good way to
achieve this, but as you observe you learn to hold yourself
apart from what you see. A reminder is needed here, however, a reminder to not observe with your mind, but with
your heart. This observance will contain a holiness, a gift of
sight beyond that of your normal vision.

You may begin by feeling compassion toward this body that   8.19
you have long viewed as your home. There it goes again, one
more time, sleeping and waking. One more time fueling
itself with energy. One more time expending that energy.
One more time growing weary. One more day is greeted,
and its greeting lies upon your heart. Each day tells you all
things come to pass. At times this is cause for rejoicing. At
other times a cause for sorrow. But never can it be evaded
that each day is a beginning and an ending both. Night is as
certain as day.

Into these days that come to pass move many other bodies   8.20
such as yours. Each one is distinct — and there are so many!
As you become an observer you may well be overwhelmed
by what you observe, by the sheer magnitude of all that with
you occupies the world. Some days this will make you feel
like one of many, a tiny peon of little significance. On other
days you will feel quite superior, the ultimate achievement of
the world and all its years of evolution. There are days you
will feel quite of the earth, as if this is your natural home and
heaven to your soul. On other days your feeling will be quite
the opposite, and you will wonder where you are. Yes, there
your body is, but where are you?

Although you cannot observe it, you will become aware of   8.21
how the past walks through your days with you, and the

future too. Both are like companions who for a little while are welcome distractions but are loath to leave you when you would have them gone.

8.22   Where lives this past and future? Where does day go when it is night? What are you to make of all these forms that wander through your days with you? What is it, really, that you are observing?

8.23   This is your reenactment of creation, begun each morning and completed each night. Each day is your creation held together by the thought system that gave it birth. To observe this is to see its reality. To see this reality is to see the image of God you have created in God's likeness. This image is based on your memory of the truth of God's creation and your desire to create like your Father. It is the best, in your forgetfulness, that you could do; but still it tells you much.

8.24   Everything is held together by the thought system that gave birth to it. There are but two thought systems: the thought system of God, and the thought system of the ego or the separated self. The thought system of the separated self sees everything in separation. The thought system of God sees everything in unity. God's thought system is one of continuous creation, rebirth, and renewal. The ego's thought system is one of continuous destruction and disassembly, of decay and death. And yet how like they are one to the other!

8.25   How like to memory it is to think a thing remembered in every smallest detail and yet to have no idea what the memory is about! All memory is twisted and distorted by what you would have it be. Everyone can think of at least one long remembered incident that when given to the light of truth revealed a lie of outlandish proportions. These are the memories of loved ones you were sure were trying to hurt you when in truth they were only trying to help. The memories of situations you deemed meant to embarrass or destroy you that were in truth meant to teach you what you needed to learn to lead you to a success you now enjoy.

Thus your memory of God's creation is a memory you retain   8.26
to the smallest detail, and yet the details mask the truth so thoroughly that all truth is given over to illusion.

How can it be that you move through the same world day   8.27
by day in the same body, observing many situations like unto each other, awakening to the same sun rising and setting, and yet can experience each day so differently that one day you feel happy and one day you feel sad, one day you feel hope and one day you feel despair? How can it be that what was created so like to God's creation can be so opposite to it? How can memory so deceive the eyes, and yet fail to deceive the heart?

This is the truth of your existence, an existence in which   8.28
your eyes deceive you but your heart believes not in the deception. Your days are but evidence of this truth. What your eyes behold will one day deceive you while what your heart beholds will the next day see through the deception. And so one day lived in your world is misery incarnate and the next a thing of joy.

Rejoice that your heart is not deceived, for herein lies your   8.29
path to true remembering.

*The lilies of the field neither
sow nor reap and yet they are provided for. The birds
of the air live to sing a song of gladness. So do you.*

— 9.32

You wonder how it can be said that your heart is not 9.1
deceived when it seems so often to deceive you. It seems as
fickle as your mind, telling you one thing one day and one
thing the next. Even more so than your mind it seems to
lead you astray, forcing you to walk through paths full of
danger and treachery into the deepest darkness instead of
toward the light. It is your emotions rather than your heart
that would do this to you.

Emotions speak the language of your separated self rather 9.2
than the language of your heart. They are the forward
guard of your defense system, always on the look out for
what might hurt or slight the *little you* that they deem
under their protection, or the other little selves you deem
under yours. But remember now how like to creation in
form if not in substance what you have made is. Creation
needs no protection, and it is only your belief in the need
for protection that has caused what you feel to become so
clouded by illusion. If you felt no need to protect your
heart, or any of those bodies that you love, your feelings

75

would retain their innocence and could not hurt you in any way.

9.3   The desire to protect is a desire that arises from distrust and is based totally on fear. If there were no fear, what would there be to protect? Thus, all of your love — the love that you imagine you keep within yourself, and the love that you imagine you receive and give — is tainted by your fear and cannot be real love. It is because you remember love as that which kept you safe, that which kept you happy, that which bound all those you love to you, that you attempt to use love here. This is a real memory of creation that you have distorted. Your faulty memory has caused you to believe love can be used to keep you safe, to make you happy and bind to you those you choose to love. This is not the case, for love cannot be used.

9.4   This is how you have distorted all relationship as well, making of it something that only becomes real in its use by you or to you. In your memory of creation you have remembered that all things exist in relationship, and that all things happen in relationship. Thus you have chosen to use relationship to prove your existence and to make things happen. This use of relationship will never provide the proof or the action you seek, because relationship cannot be used.

9.5   Look around the room in which you sit and take away the usefulness from each thing you see in it. How many items would you keep that you now look upon? Your body too was created for its usefulness. It sets you apart, just as each item in your room is set apart by what it is useful for. Ask yourself now: To whom is your body useful? This question does not apply to those for whom you cook or clean, those whose bodies you would repair or minds improve. The question is, really, who might have seen a use for a body such as yours before it was created? What kind of creator would create it and for what purpose?

You did not create your Self, but your body you did create.   9.6
It was created for its usefulness just like every other object
that shares the space you occupy. Think for a moment of
what the creator of such a body would have intended the
body to be. The body is a finite entity, created to be self-contained but also to self-destruct. It was created with a need for
constant maintenance, a maintenance that requires toil and
struggle. Every inch of its surface is a receiver and transmit-
ter of information yet it carries additional tools such as eyes
and ears to enhance its communication and to control what
goes in and what goes out. It is as susceptible to pain as to
pleasure. It contains the means for joining, but for joining
that is of a temporary nature. It is as capable of violence as
gentleness. It is born and dies in a state of helplessness.

The body could not help but be thus, as it was made with   9.7
dual purposes in mind. It was made to make real and then
glorify a separated self, and it was made to punish that separated self for the separation. Its creator had in mind what is
reflected in the body: self-aggrandizement and self-efface-
ment, pleasure and pain, violence and gentleness. A desire to
know everything but only through its own effort, a desire
to see everything but only through its own eyes, a desire to be
known but only through what it would choose to share.
Alongside these desires it is easy to see how a world such as
that of the body developed. Alongside the desire to know was
the desire not to know. Alongside the desire to see was the
desire not to see. Alongside the desire to share was the desire
to be hidden. Alongside the desire to live was the desire to live
no more.

You have always been as you were created, but this is what   9.8
you chose to make from that with which you started. In
other words, you took what you are and made this of yourself. You did not create something from nothing and you did
not usurp the power of God. You took what God created

and turned it into an illusion so powerful that you believe it is what you are, rather than believing in the truth. But just as you have done this, you can undo this. This is the choice set before you — to go on believing in the illusion you have made, or to begin to see the truth.

9.9   Now you seek to know how to escape what you have made. To do so you must withdraw all faith from it. This you are not ready yet to do, but this is what your heart will now prepare you for. As you are prepared, you walk alongside him who has waited for you with a single purpose instead of alongside the conflicting desires you chose to let lead you to this strange world. You travel lightly now where before you walked in chains. You travel now with a companion who knows you as you are and would show your Self to you.

9.10   Look upon your body now as you earlier looked upon the space you occupy. Take away the body's usefulness. Would you keep that which you now look upon? As you stand back and observe your body, always with the vision of your heart, think about just what it is that you would use it for. What God created cannot be used, but what you have made can, for its only purpose is your use. Choose to use it now to return you to your real Self, and the new purpose you establish will change its conditions as well as its usefulness to you.

9.11   All use is predicated on the simple idea that you do not have what you need. You will continue to believe this while your allegiance remains split. Until you have withdrawn all faith in what you have made, you will believe that what you made remains useful to you. Since this is the case, and since it cannot be changed without your total willingness to change it — a willingness not yet complete — we will, instead of trying to ignore what you have made, use it in a new way. Keep in mind, however, that we are merely saving time, and that your real Self has no need to use anything at all.

As stated before, what is most useful to us now is your per- 9.12
ception of your heart. Your illusions concerning it, when undone, will quickly reveal to you the truth because your misperceptions concerning your heart remain closer to the truth than any that you hold. The memories of your heart are the strongest and purest that exist, and their remembrance will help to still your mind and reveal the rest.

We thus return to your perception of your emotions and all 9.13
that causes you to feel. In your feelings, especially those you cannot name, lie your connection to all that is. This is useful because what you have named and classified is harder to dislodge and bring to light. Even those feelings you attempt to name and keep cleverly in a box that you have labeled this or that often are not content to stay where you would place them. They seem to betray you, when it is you who betray them by not allowing them to be what they are. This could be used as a capsule definition of your entire problem: You do not allow anything that exists in your world, including yourself, to be what it is.

Feelings that on their own seem to rebel against this insane 9.14
situation are guided by memories trying to reveal the truth to you. They call to you from a place that you know not. The difficulty is that the only self that is listening to this call is your separated self. It is in the attempts of the separated self to interpret what feelings would say that they become as distorted as all the rest. It is the separated self that feels impelled to label feelings good and bad, some worthy of acknowledgment and the rest worthy only of denial or contempt. It is your language that gives emotion its place, one

step behind fear, in your battle to control or protect what you have made.

9.15   Fear always lies one step beneath the surface of a situation because it lies one step beneath the surface of your self. Peel back the first level of what your eyes allow you to observe and you will find fear lurking there. The next level, depending on your disposition, is either the desire to control or the desire to protect. They are really the same but they wear different faces to the world. If, for the purposes of our discussion, the body is the surface aspect of your self, and if beneath that surface what is first encountered is fear, it is from fear that all the rest proceeds. Surely it is easy to see that neither the desire to control nor to protect would exist without the layer of fear that comes before it.

9.16   Fear, like all the rest of your emotions, comes in many guises and is given many names, but there are really only two emotions: one is fear, the other love. Fear is thus the source of all illusion, love the source of truth.

9.17   How could one separated off from all the rest not be fearful? It matters not at all that all whom you observe seem to be separate as well. No one really believes another to be as separate as he is. It always seems as if others have what you lack and what you are looking for. You seem to be alone in your frailty, loneliness, and lack of love. Others misunderstand you and know you not, and neither can you make any sense of them.

9.18   This need not be, for you are not separate! The relationships you seek to end your loneliness can do so if you but learn to see relationship differently. As with all your problems in perception, fear is what blocks the vision of your heart, the light the Christ in you would shine upon the darkness. Can you not see that when you chose to make yourself separate and alone you also made the choice for fear? Fear is nothing but a choice, and it can be replaced by choice of another kind.

It has been said often that cause and effect are one in truth. 9.19 The world you see is the effect of fear. Each one of you would have compassion for a child tormented by nightmares. Each parent's most fervent wish would be to tell a child truthfully there is no cause for fear. Age has not taken fear from any of you nor made your dream of life any less of a nightmare. Yet you spare few moments of compassion for yourself, and when such chance occurrences come about you quickly override compassion with practicality. While it makes sense to you to attempt to dispel a child's nightmare, you see no way to dispel your own. You hide fear beneath the surface, and behind each alternate label you would give it, in a desperate attempt to see it not. To live in fear is, indeed, a curse, and one that you would try to tell yourself is not present in your life. You look to others to feel compassion for, to those living in countries torn by war or neighborhoods steeped in violence. There is cause for fear, you say. But not here.

This is the only way you have been able to see to bring relief 9.20 to the nightmare of a life of fear. You project fear outward and away from yourself, seeing not that you keep that which you would project. Seeing not that outward signs of fear are but reflections of what you keep within.

Think now of one of those you have identified as living the 9.21 life of fear you deny yourself. And imagine that you could bring this one in from that dark and dangerous place. She is cold, and you prepare a fire and give her a warm blanket for her knees. He is hungry and you prepare a feast for him fit to serve a king. This one exists in the violence you would keep outside your doors, and from your inner sanctum you give this one a respite from the war that rages beyond it. All of your behavior and even your fantasies testify that you believe an absence of cold makes for warmth. That the absence of hunger is fullness. The absence of violence peace. You think that if you but provide these things that are opposite to what you would not want to have, you have accomplished much. But a warm fire will only provide warmth as long as it is stoked. A meal will provide fullness only until the next is needed. Your closed door only keeps you safe while its boundary is respected. To replace the temporary with the temporary is not an answer.

9.22   You may be thinking now that what I have just told you is not an answer is precisely what the Bible has instructed you to do. I am recorded as telling you to feed the hungry, to quench the thirst of the thirsty, to welcome and give rest to the stranger. I have said when you do this unto others you do this to me. Do you think that I am in need of a meal, a cup of water, a warm bed? While you are trapped in the illusion of need surely these acts of charity are of some value, but again I tell you that this value is temporary. My words call you to the eternal, to nourishment and rest of the spirit rather than the body. That your sights are set on the care of the body alone is another example of choosing an opposite for replacement.

9.23   Is this not your way of solving all the problems that you face? You see what you do not want and try to replace it with its opposite. Your life is thus spent in struggling against what you have for what you have not. Only one example is needed to clarify the predicament you have placed yourself in. You feel lacking and so you want. You want and want and want. You truly believe you do not have what you need, and so make yourself continuously needy. You thus spend your life trying to fulfill your needs. For most of you, this trying takes on the form of work and you spend your entire life working to meet your needs and those of the ones you love. What would you do with your life if you had no needs to meet? What would you do with your life if you had no fear? These questions are the same.

The only replacement that can occur that will accomplish   9.24
what you seek is the replacement of illusion with the truth, the replacement of fear with love, the replacement of your separated self with your real Self, the Self that rests in unity. It is your knowledge that this must occur that leads you to attempt every other kind of replacement. You can continue on in this fashion, always hoping that the next replacement will be the one that succeeds in bringing you what you desire, or you can choose instead the only replacement that will work.

All that you are asked to give up is your insane notion that   9.25
you are alone. We speak much of your body here only because it is your proof of this insane idea's validity. It is your proof as well that a life of fear is warranted. How could you not fear for the safety of a home as fragile as the body? How could you fail to provide the next meal for yourself and those within your care? You do not see all that these distractions of meeting needs would keep you from.

And yet the very reality that you have set up — the reality   9.26
of not being able to succeed in what you must constantly strive to do — is a situation set up to provide relationship. Like everything else you have remembered of creation and made in its image, so too is this. While making yourself separate and alone you have also made it necessary to be in relationship to survive. Without relationship your *species* itself would cease to be, in fact, all life would end. Of course you

must help your sister and brother, for they are yourself, and they are your only means to grasp eternity even within this false reality you have made.

9.27   Let us return to the example of feeding your sister's hunger and quenching your brother's thirst. This is not only a lesson in feeding and quenching spiritual hunger and thirst, but a lesson in relationship as well. It is the relationship inherent in meeting another's need that makes the meeting of the need a thing of lasting value. It is your willingness to say, "Brother, you are not alone" that is the benefit of such situations, not only to your brother but also to you. It is in saying, "Sister, you are not alone" that spiritual hunger and thirst is met with the fullness of unity. It is in realizing that you are not alone that you realize your unity with me and begin to turn from fear toward love.

9.28   You are not your own creator. This is your salvation. You did not create something from nothing, and what you started with is what God created and remains as God created it. You do not have to ask yourself to stretch your belief beyond these simple statements. Are they really so implausible as to be beyond your acceptance? Is it so impossible to imagine that what God created was distorted by your desire to have your reality be other than what it is? Have you not seen this kind of distortion take place within the reality you do see? Is this not the story of the gifted son or daughter who squanders all the gifts he or she possesses by seeing them not or by sadly distorting what they might be useful for?

9.29   You are the prodigal sons and daughters welcomed constantly to return home to your Father's safe embrace.

9.30   Think of your automobile or computer or any other *thing* you use. Without a user, would it have any function at all?

Would it be anything? An automobile abandoned and without a user might become the home to a family of mice. A computer might be covered with a cloth, a flowerpot placed on top of it. Someone not knowing what it is for would make of it what he or she would have it be, but never would the user seek to exchange roles with it. When an accident happens, an automobile cannot be seen to be at fault for mistakes made by its user. Yet in a way this exchange of roles is similar to what you have attempted to do and it is like placing the blame for a car accident on the automobile. You have attempted to change places with the body, claiming that it is using you rather than that you are using it. You do so out of guilt in an attempt to place your guilt outside yourself. "My body made me do it" is like the cry of the child with an imaginary friend. With his claim of an imaginary friend, the child announces that his body is not within his control. What is your ego but an imaginary friend to you?

9.31   Child of God, you need no imaginary friend when you have beside you he who is your friend always and he who would show you that you have no needs at all. What you truly are cannot be used, not even by God. See you not that it is only in illusion that you can use others who are like yourself?

9.32   You learn your concept of using others from the reality you have made in which you use the body that you call your home and identify as your own self. How can the user and the object of use be one and the same? This insanity makes the purpose of your life seem to be one of usefulness. The more your body can be of use to others and to yourself, the more worthwhile you see it as being. Ages have passed since creation began, and still you have not learned the lesson of the birds of the air or the flowers of the field. Two thousand years have passed since you were told to observe this lesson. The lilies of the field neither sow nor reap and yet they are provided for. The birds of the air live to sing a song of gladness. So do you.

9.33   God's will for you is happiness, and never has it been otherwise. God's creation is for eternity and has no use for time. Time too is of your making, an idea of use gone mad, as once again you have taken something made for your own use and allowed it to become the user. With your own two hands you give away all your happiness and power to that which you have made! It matters little now that in so doing you once again imitated what your faulty memory would tell you that your creator did. God alone can give free will. In giving your power to things like your body and to ideas like time your imitation of the gift of free will is so falsely placed in illusion that you cannot see this madness for what it truly is. Your body has no use for your power, and time was not made for happiness.

9.34   The free will that God gave you is what has allowed you to make of yourself and your world what you will. Now you look upon this world with guilt and see it as evidence of your evil nature. It reinforces your belief that you have changed too much from what you were to ever again be worthy of your true inheritance. You fear that this, too, you would squander and lay to ruin. The only thing that might succeed in proving your place as that of royal inheritor would be if you could fix yourself and the world, restoring it to a previous condition that you imagine you know. In this scenario God is like unto your banker rather than your Father. You would prove to God that you can "make a go of it" before you would ask Him for His help.

9.35   As long as you do not want to be forgiven you will not feel the gentle touch of forgiveness upon you and your world.

While there is no need in truth for this forgiveness, as there is no truth to this big change that you believe you have undergone, your desire to be forgiven is a first step away from your belief that you can fix things by yourself and in so doing earn your way back into your Father's home. Being willing to be forgiven is the precursor of atonement, the state in which you allow your errors to be corrected for you. These errors are not the sins you hold against yourself, but merely your errors in perception. Correction, or atonement, returns you to your natural state where true vision lies and error and sin disappear.

Your natural state is one of union, and each joining that you 9.36 do in holy relationship returns a little of the memory of union to you. This memory of your divinity is what you seek in truth from each special relationship you enter into, but your true quest is hidden by the concept of use that gets in its way. While your heart seeks for union, your separated self seeks for what it can use to fill the emptiness and ease the terror of its separation. What your heart seeks in love it attains, but your separated self would keep this attainment from you by turning every situation into a means to serve its ends. As long as union is seen as a means only to keep loneliness from you it is not seen for what it truly is.

You have placed limits on all things in your world, and it is 9.37 these limits of usefulness that would block your memory's return. A love relationship, while seen as the ultimate achievement in terms of the closeness you can acquire with a brother or sister, is still limited by what you would have it do. Its purpose, simply stated, is to supply a lack. This is your definition of completion. What is missing in you is found in another and together a sense of wholeness is achieved.

9.38   Again this is but a distortion of creation. You remember that wholeness is achieved through union, but not how to accomplish it. You have forgotten that only you can be accomplished. You believe that by putting various parts together a whole can be achieved. You speak of balance, and try to find something for one part of yourself in one place and something for another somewhere else. This one fulfills your need for friendship and that one for intellectual stimulation. In one activity you express your creativity and in another your prayerfulness. Like a diversified investment portfolio, you think this parceling out of different aspects of yourself protects your assets. You fear "putting all your eggs in one basket." You seek to balance the things you label drudgery and the things you label exciting. In doing so you see yourself as "spending your time" wisely, and you call yourself a "well-rounded individual." As long as more than this is not sought, more than this will not be realized.

9.39   Seeking what you have lost in other people, places, and things is but a sign that you do not understand that what you have lost still belongs to you. What you have lost is missing, not gone. What you have lost is hidden to you but has not disappeared nor ceased to be. What you have lost is valuable indeed, and this you know. But you know not what this valuable something is. One thing alone is sure: When you have found it you will know that it has been found. This is what will bring you happiness and peace, contentment and a sense of belonging. This is what will cause you to feel as if your time here has not been in vain. You know that whatever else your life seems to be for, if on your deathbed you have not found what you have sought, you will not leave in deepest peace but in dark despair and fear. You will have no hope for what lies *beyond* life, for you will have found no hope *in* life.

Your quest for what is missing thus becomes the race you 9.40
run against death. You seek it here, you seek it there, and
scurry on to the next thing and the next. Each person runs
this race alone, with hope only of victory for himself. You
realize not that if you were to stop and take your brother's
hand, the racecourse would become a valley full of lilies, and
you would find your Self on the other side of the finish line,
able at last to rest.

The injunction to rest in peace is for the living, not the 9.41
dead. But while you run the race you will know it not.
Competition that leads to individual achievement has
become the idol you would glorify, and you need not look
far for evidence that this is so. This idolatry tells you that
glory is for the few, and so you take your place in line at the
starting gate and make your bid for glory. You run the race
as long as you can and, win or lose, your participation in the
race was but the required offering to the idol you have made.
And at some point, when you can run the race no more, you
bow down to those who have achieved glory; they become
your idols and you become their subjects, watching what
they do with envy and with awe. To these you make your
sacrifices and pay your homage. To these you say, "I would
be like you." To these you look for a vicarious fulfillment,
having given up any hope for real fulfillment. Here you are
entertained, shocked, excited, or repelled. Here you watch
the gladiators kill one another for your amusement. Here is
your notion of use displayed in all its most horrific detail.

What is this but a demonstration, on a larger scale, of what 9.42
you live each day? This is all that anything larger than yourself demonstrates to you. All society, groups, teams, and
organizations are but a collective portrayal of individual
desire. Slaves and masters but use one another and the same
laws bind both. Who is master and who is slave in this body

you would call your home? What freedom would you have without the demands your body places upon you? The same question can be asked of this world you see as home to the body. Which is master and which is slave when both are held in bondage? The glory you give idols is but bondage as well. Without your idolatry their glory would be no more, and so they live in fear no less than that of those who idolize them.

9.43   Use, in any form, leads to bondage, and so to perceive a world based on use is to see a world where freedom is impossible. What you think you need your sister for is thus based upon this insane premise that freedom can be purchased and that master is freer than slave. Although this is illusion, it is the illusion that is sought. The purchase price is usefulness. And so each joining is seen as a bartering in which you trade your usefulness for that of another. An employer has use for your skills and you have use for the salary and benefits the employer offers. A spouse is useful in many ways that complement your areas of usefulness. A store provides you with goods that you would use, and you supply a store with capital that its owner will use. If you are gifted with beauty or athletic or artistic talent that can be used, how lucky you think you are. A beautiful face and a fit body can be traded for so much. It is no secret that you live in a world of supply and demand. From the simple concept of individuals needing to be in relationship to survive has grown this complex web of use and abuse.

9.44   Abuse is but improper use — use on a scale that makes the insanity of use obvious to both the user and the usee, and so has its proper place in our discussion here. Look at patterns of abuse, in everything from drugs and alcohol to physical or emotional mistreatment. These, like the larger examples of your daily life gone awry, are but demonstrations of internal desires taken to a greater extreme; only these, rather than being reflected by the group, are reflected within the individual. The individual with issues of abuse would do a service to the world if the people in it were to understand what that abuse is a reflection of. Like any extreme, it merely points out what in less extreme instances is still the same: Use is improper.

It is its purpose that makes use improper. The Holy Spirit   9.45
can guide you to use the things that you have made in ways that benefit the whole, and this is the distinction between proper and improper use, or use and abuse. You would use for the benefit of the separated self. When magnified, the destructive force of such abuse is easily apparent. Again you would place the blame outside yourself and label drugs, alcohol, tobacco, gambling, and even food as destructive forces. Like the automobile you would blame for an accident, user and usee have become confused. All such confusion stems from the initial confusion of the use you think your body would put you to. All such confusion stems from your displacement of yourself and your abdication of your power to the things that you have made.

Let me say again that this is your misguided attempt to fol-   9.46
low in creation's way. God gave all power to his creations, and you would choose to do this as well. Your intent is not evil, but is guided by the guilt and false remembering of the separated self. As much as you have desired anonymity and autonomy from God, still you blame God for creating a situation in which you think you have been allowed to hurt yourself. How could God allow all this suffering, you ask? Why does He tempt you with such destructive forces? Forces beyond your control? Why did not God create a world benign and unable to harm you?

9.47   Such is the world that God did create: A world so lovely and so peaceful that when you see it once again you will cry with joy and forget your sadness in an instant. There will be no long remembering of regrets, no feeling badly for all the years in which you saw this not. There will merely be a glad "Aha!" as what was long forgotten is returned to you. You will but smile at the childish games you played, and have no more regrets than you would have for your childhood. Your innocence will stand out clearly here, and never again will you doubt that the world that God created belongs to you and you to it.

9.48   All your vast wanderings will be seen for what they are. All that you desired will be revealed as only two desires, the desire to love and the desire to be loved. Why wait to see that these desires are all that call you to the strange behavior you display? Those who give in to abuse are merely calling louder for the selfsame love that all are in search of. Judgment is not due them, for all here are abusers — starting with their own selves.

9.49   Attempts to modify the behavior of abuse are near to useless in a world based on use. The foundation of the world must change, and the stimulus for this change lies within you. All use ends with joining, for use is what you have traded joining for. Instead of recognizing your union, a state in which you are whole and complete because you are joined with all, you have determined to stand separate and use the rest to support your separate stance. Do you see the difference in these two positions? In what way is your way better than the way God created for you, a way that is completely free of conflict? Despite your bravest attempts to remain separate, you must use your brothers and sisters in order to even maintain the illusion of your separation. Would it not simply be better to end this charade? To admit that you were not created for separation but for union? To begin to let go of your fear of joining, and as you do let go of use as well?

How different would the world be if you would but attempt for one day to replace use with union! Before you can begin, however, we must expand on the lessons you are learning by observing your own self. Now we seek to uncover the illusion that you can be used by your body, for your own seeming use by such as this leads to all other ideas of use.

A door has been reached, a threshold crossed. What your mind still would deny your heart cannot. A tiny glimmering of memory has returned to you and will not leave you to the chaos you seem to prefer. — 10.32

First let us consider what it is the body would use. Although you feel slave to it and under the weight of its control, who is the you it would control? How can it make you do other than you choose to do? Learn this lesson well, for herein lies the cure to all disease and the hope of all healing. While the body seems to tell you what you feel and bid you act in accordance with its feelings, how can this be so? The body by itself is neutral. But as long as you attribute the body with bringing you pleasure, the body will bring you pain as well. You cannot choose one without the other, because the choice is the same. The body is a tool made for your use in maintaining the illusion of your separation. That it has seeming power can only be because you think you put your power there. If this were true, much power indeed would it wield. But what you have made cannot be invested with the power of creation without your joining with it. How, you think, could you be more linked with anything than you are with your own body? If you are not even joined with this presence that you call your home, how can you be expected to join with others?

10.1

95

10.2   Now we must return to the concept of relationship, for the thought of bodies joined in union closer than the union that you feel with the body you call your own is indeed ridiculous. Joining happens in relationship, not in physical form. Joining is not the obliteration of one thing to make another — joining makes each one whole, and in this wholeness one with all. This union has never really ceased to be, but as long as you do not realize that it exists its benefits are unavailable to you. As much as I would like it to be so, my telling you the truth of your existence is not enough of itself to make you aware of what you have for so long hidden from yourself. I can merely tell you where to look, and save you countless years of seeking where the truth is not, if you will but seek where I bid you find.

10.3   There are aspects of what I am telling you that you readily embrace and others that you do not understand and would wait awhile before implementing. What you truly do not understand is wholeness. All things exist in wholeness, including the thought system that you made to protect the illusion you hold so dear. Your thought system is completely alien to the truth, but completely consistent as a system. You cannot abandon one tenet and retain another because by retaining part you retain all. This will lead to seeming failure to learn what I would have you learn. What God would have me teach, you cannot fail to learn, but neither can you learn of it in parts. The thought system of truth is as wholly consistent as the thought system of illusion, and you cannot take what you will and leave the rest. Thus we will continue to point out the differences in the two thought systems so that your ideas can begin to change, until finally your heart takes over and makes the one choice you are bound to make. Your heart — not to be confused with the pump that runs the body, but identified as the center of yourself — has no thought system separate from your own and must exist in the reality where you think you are.

The beginning of all transformation is at the source, and this 10.4 is as true of illusion as of the truth. You see your body as your self, and your self as source of all that you have done and felt in all your days upon this earth. Yet your real source is at the center of your Self, the altar to your Creator, the Self you share in unity with Christ. Christ is the "part" of God that resides in you, not in separation but in the eternal wholeness in which God and you together exist in truth.

For those of you who have been journeying long, as well as 10.5 those of you just beginning, this abandonment of the body as your home and source of all you are is the greatest hurdle to overcome. As you observe the body and dare to think of life without it, you again and again encounter its reality. When its awareness begins to leave you is just when you may be beset by headaches, back pain, and other seeming maladies. This is the separated self that you have made calling you back to the body to prove to you that it is insurmountable. Many people at this point try to think these maladies away, and when they do not succeed they see this as further evidence of their entrenchment in the body. Beware all attempts to think the body away and to think miracles into existence. This desire merely shows you know not the source of healing and are not ready to be healed.

That you are not ready yet does not mean you will not be 10.6 ready, just as having lost something does not mean it no longer exists. Yet your separated self would cite all evidence of its failure to be other than separate and be quick to point out to you the impossibility of being other than what you are — a body. This is the "fact" it whispers constantly in your ear, the lie that it would have you believe makes all else you would learn here as impossible as this. You listen to this voice because it has been your constant companion and teacher in your separation, not realizing that what it has taught you is to be separate. Be warned that it will constantly try to interfere as long as you place any merit in what it tells you.

10.7 Think of another, a teacher or a parent, whose "voice" you hear as you go through your days. Whether you want to hear this voice or not, whether this voice was wise or foolish, the very repetition of this voice keeps it in your memory. This may be the voice that says, "Stand up straight," or "You're special," or "You will never amount to anything." Many of you may have used therapy to still the negative messages that you hear, and after much effort succeeded at replacing what was negative with messages of a more positive nature. And these are but messages of an outside source! Your own thoughts are much more persistent and insistent than these. They have been with you longer and more constantly. Vigilance is needed to dislodge them.

10.8 I tell you this not to discourage you, but to encourage you not to give up. Your purpose now is the holiest possible and all of heaven is with you. All that is needed is your continuing willingness. All that can cause you to fail is giving up. I give you these examples that will make you say, "It will not be easy," but I tell you neither will it be hard if you but remember this: your willingness is all that is needed. When your separated self whispers to you, "Your body is but a fact," all you need tell yourself is, "I am still willing to believe otherwise."

10.9 Be aware also of your desire for reward. As you feel yourself becoming closer to God and your true Self, as you gain more awareness of yourself as a "good" person and one trying to be better still, you will begin to look for your rewards. Later you will look back upon this time and smile and laugh out loud at the innocence of these desires that but reveal that you stand merely at the beginning of the curriculum. To want a reward for goodness, for trying harder, for being closer to God than your brother or sister, are all desires of your separated self wanting something for itself and all its effort. This is but a stage you will pass through, though some may linger long here. You will stay until you realize that all are good and that you cannot earn more of God's good graces than your brother. You will stay until you realize that God has given everything already to everyone.

Again but state your willingness. A willingness to believe that you have everything you need despite the "fact" that it does not seem so. Your willingness is all that is needed to move you through this stage and to the next. Be encouraged rather than discouraged that God does not grant all your desires here. For these are not yet your true desires, and the rewards you would choose here are as dust to those you will become aware of as you proceed.   10.10

Let us talk a moment here of miracles. Simply stated, miracles are a natural consequence of joining. Magic is your attempt to do miracles "on your own." In the early stages of your learning, you will be tempted to play a game of make-believe. You will not believe that you are not your body, but you would make believe that you are not. You may then be tempted to believe that because you are pretending you are not a body, you can pretend you do not feel the pain of a headache or the cold of a winter day, and this pretending may even make you feel a little less pain or a little less cold. But this attempt to fool yourself is welcomed by your separated self who knows pretending will not make it so.   10.11

10.12   These attempts to fool yourself are based on your lack of understanding rather than your lack of belief. You would not still be reading if you believed you were your body and that alone. Long have you known that there is more to you than flesh and bones. Belief is not your problem. Understanding is. While you believe in God, you do not understand God. While you believe in me, you do not understand how these words have come from me. While you believe in heaven and an afterlife, you do not understand what or where they are. And to believe in something that you do not understand makes you feel peculiar at the least and delusional at the worst. You want to believe and so you believe. But you also want to be "right" about what you believe. The convenient thing about your belief in God, in me, in heaven, and in an afterlife is that you do not think you will be proven wrong here. If you are wrong, you will merely rot away after you have died and no one will know how wrong you were! If you are wrong, at least you believed in something that brought you comfort and in the end did you no harm.

10.13   This is not as easily said about the concept of not being separate, however. The only thing you find really difficult to believe is that you are in union with your brothers and sisters, right now, today. To believe in God without understanding God is one thing. To believe in your union with your neighbor without understanding either union or your neighbor is something else. This belief will not necessarily bring you comfort or do you no harm. What if you believe in the goodness of your neighbor and that belief is unwarranted? What if you are trusting and find that trust to be misplaced? What if you are simply naive and are taken for a fool? What if you are wrong?

10.14   A similar fear strikes your heart when you consider giving up your belief in the body. To believe you are not your body while you walk around within it is something quite different than believing in God. Here all the proof available would say that you are wrong. All the proof of your eyes and ears, as well as that of science, would say you *are* your body. Even history would seem to prove this fact as you look back and say even Jesus died before he could rise again as spirit.

I am here to teach you once again because I was the example life. Do you believe that when I walked the earth I was a body, or do you believe that I was the Son of God before I was born into human form, during the time I existed in human form, and after I rose again? This is rightly called the mystery of faith: Christ has died, Christ has risen, Christ will come again. What is missing from this recitation? Christ was born. Nowhere in the mystery of faith is it stated that Christ became a body. 10.15

You have not been told that the body does not exist, only that it is not you. Like all tools you made, it is illusion because you have no need of tools. But while you believe you do, it is quite real to you. To give up the body entirely is a choice you need not make. As your learning advances you will see that this is possible, but there may be reasons not to choose this. At this point, however, all that is asked is that your body is seen as what it is — both in terms of what you made it for and in terms of the way in which you can now be guided to use it for the benefit of all. 10.16

The choice for many has seemed to be "Would you rather be right or happy?" Only the ego would choose being right over happiness. As you observe your body, also observe its actions in terms of the choices it makes. Ask yourself, "What choice may have led to this situation or event?" For choice is always involved *before* the fact. Nothing happens to the Son of God by accident. This observation will help to put the 10.17

responsibility of your life back into your hands, where it belongs. You are not helpless, nor are you at the whim of forces beyond your control. The only force beyond your control is your own mind, and this need not be. When you begin to ask yourself, What choice might lead to happiness instead of this, you will begin to see a difference in your body's response to what appear to be external events, and then a change in the external events themselves.

10.18   Your mind might still prefer to be right rather than happy, so it is important that you let your heart lead in making this new choice. When you find yourself in a situation you do not like, again offer your willingness to find some happiness within it. These instructions to your heart will begin to make a difference to your state of mind.

10.19   What you would call your state of mind is more like a general atmosphere, an ambiance, a mood — and this setting is determined with your heart. The thoughts of your separated self care little for such as this and would call such concerns irrelevant to its well-being. Its survival *as it is* is its only concern. This is not just concern for needs such as food and shelter, but for survival of the thought system of the separated self. Happiness is not a priority here, but being right is quite important to it. It would prefer to be serious and heavy hearted rather than light hearted and gay. Being serious about life is a major strategy of the separated self, which recognizes its own seriousness as necessary to maintain its separation. Joy is truly the greatest threat to the separated self, for it comes from union and reinforces union's appeal at the expense of the appeal of separation.

10.20   You do not realize how quickly the separated self rushes in to sabotage all movement away from separation and toward union. Many of you have recognized that you seem to minimize your chances for happiness and maximize your chances for unhappiness through the choices you would make. You look back longingly at times of happiness and wonder what went wrong and why you could not maintain that happy state. There might be many practical reasons to cite for your happiness' demise, but in the loneliness that comes with its loss you will wonder, at least briefly, why the choice for practicality needed to be made. Yet if the separated self can look back and see that it chose being right over being happy, it will congratulate itself despite its unhappiness and say, "I did the right thing." It will see itself as victor over the foolish dreams of happiness and say how glad it is that it came to its senses before it was too late.

Each of you is aware of a threshold you would cross that leaves no route open for return. That threshold is often a happiness so fulfilling that once you have experienced it you say, "I will take this despair no more." For others this threshold is the opposite, an experience of pain so great that they would rather die than continue on in such a way. Addicts too but choose a different threshold wherein after experiencing the oblivion of the separated self through drugs, alcohol, or even constant work or shopping, they refuse to return to the separated self's reality. If they cannot leave it, they will block it out. Some, at this threshold, turn back. They deny themselves the joy or the pain or the oblivion that would make return impossible and count themselves lucky for not going to the place from which change would become inevitable.   10.21

The separated self is so ensconced in fear that the known fears of its existence seem preferable to the unknown fears of any other kind of existence. That an option could be chosen that leaves no room for fear at all does not occur to it, for the absence of fear is something it has never known.   10.22

10.23　If the body is the surface aspect of your existence and fear lies beneath the surface, see the advantage of this exercise: Place your body out in front of yourself where you can be its silent observer. As you watch your hands go about their work or the shadow form on the ground as you walk to and fro, you will be learning the only separation that can be useful to you.

10.24　Your first realization of significance will be that all you hear does not come through your ears. You will find that you are full of thoughts — thoughts *about* your body, the same kind of thoughts you might have of someone else's body. The difference will be that these thoughts will not seem to have originated in your head. You may realize for the first time or in a different way that you have always heard your thoughts without the benefit of your ears. You may be saying now, "Of course that is the way we hear our thoughts — it is the nature of thought." But have you ever before considered the nature of your thoughts, or have you merely taken them for granted?

10.25　Thoughts are not seen nor heard and yet they are with you constantly, and never more so than as you conduct your experiment in detachment from the body. This is why we conduct this experiment. Whether you term yourself successful or a hopeless failure at conducting this experiment, you will realize anew that your thoughts more accurately define who you are than your body does. Whether they wander aimlessly or are quite focused, your thoughts are more the source of all you are and all you do than is the body you observe.

10.26　You may laugh at yourself for taking part in this silly experiment, but you will realize the desire to laugh at yourself is quite genuine and not conceived from meanness. There will be a happier self who seems to think this game is rather fun, and who is not at all concerned with the game's success. This laughter too, as well as the sense of fun that prompted it, will come without the body's participation.

You will soon develop an ability to see without your body's eyes. This, too, will seem like a silly game at first, a trick of your imagination. You will, at first, observe only that which you can "see"— your arms and legs, your shadow falling as you walk — but more and more you will come to see the body as a whole. You will see it from behind as you follow it about its day, without, at first, even being aware that this is happening. And you will find that as you observe, you are more aware of your surroundings, and more aware that your body is part of everything that is happening. There is your body and six more crossing the street. There is your body sitting at a desk in a building with many others. You will realize how seldom before you were aware of the street you walked down, of the buildings it traveled between, of the open sky above, of all the "others" traveling it with you. You will feel more a part of everything rather than less, and be surprised by this feeling. 10.27

Keep going now for this is but a beginning. Experiment, just for the fun of it, without allowing room for discouragement. This is not a test and you cannot fail. You are merely play-ing: Play at observing yourself from above. Can you look "down" upon yourself? And can you skip along and get in front to see your body coming toward you? 10.28

This body that you claim to be your "self" is but a form — how can it be that you can see it not? 10.29

What you will be feeling as you proceed is the feeling of the tunnel vision of the separated self giving way to the expanded 10.30

vision of the unified Self. As you "feel" this happening, you will begin to be aware of feelings too that are not bound to the body. Like the thoughts you neither see nor hear with your body's eyes or ears, these feelings too will not depend upon your body's senses.

10.31   You will find quite a bit of resistance to this experiment. You will find you are too serious to play this game and that you have better things to do. Yet as much as you resist, the idea has been planted and you will find yourself, at times that seem to be "against your will," participating in it despite your determination not to do so. Once you begin to feel the effects of the experiment you will also encounter fear, especially if you take the game too seriously. There will be times when you will not want to laugh when the urge to do so comes upon you, and other times that after the slightest moment of expanded vision you will welcome back your tunnel vision with gratitude. You will feel relieved that your feet still touch the ground and that the boundary of your body is still intact. But you will remember the urge to laugh gently at yourself and the expanded vision as well. You will remember that for a moment your body did not seem to be a boundary that kept you contained within its limitations. Then you will remember that this is a but a course in remembering and that memory is the language of the heart.

10.32   Many of you will rebel here thinking this is not what you signed on for. You just want to read about this course, perhaps, and not be required to take it. You will want to keep it theoretical and not apply it. You will ask for the information, and say you would really rather not have the experience. You wanted but the travelers' guide and not the actual journey. This is what too many of you sought, and many of you still resist realizing that you got more than you bargained for. A door has been reached, a threshold crossed.

What your mind still would deny your heart cannot. A tiny   10.33
glimmering of memory has returned to you and will not
leave you to the chaos you seem to prefer. It will keep calling you to acknowledge it and let it grow. It will tug at your
heart in the most gentle of ways. Its whisper will be heard
within your thoughts. Its melody will play within your
mind. "Come back, come back," it will say to you. "Come
home, come home," it will sing. You will know there is a
place within yourself where you are missed and longed for
and safe and loved. A little peace has been made room for in
the house of your insanity.

What willingness is it that you are asked to give? It can come in many manners and be given many forms. It can be called a willingness to change your mind, or to allow yourself to be open to new possibilities. It can be called a change of heart, or a willingness but to, for a little while, withdraw your fear and your protection from it. But what this willingness really does is allow your call to be sounded, your call to love and to be loved. It is a willingness to receive love from your Source and to be loved for who you are. Is this so much to ask? — 11.15

The exercises in this Course of Love are few, and they are 11.1 contained within the Course itself rather than separated from it. There are but a few reasons for this method. The first is your attitude toward instruction, and the fact that you do not really desire it. What you desire is what cannot be given from anywhere but your own source. Again you realize this aspect of creation, and it has helped to solidify your stance against union and your lack of desire for instruction. This is due to your confusion about your source. All of your fierce determination to hang on to your individuality stems from this confusion. If your source were truly your body and the brain that causes it to function, then you would indeed be required to learn things "on your own," for all true learning must come from your source.

You think your source and your creator are two separate 11.2 things, and too seldom remember even that you are not your own creator. You have made this separation based on the idea that what created you cannot be one with you. Again this only points to your lack of recognition of what creation really is. And yet when you would practice creativity you realize it is a celebration of the creator — and when you honor artists of all kinds you honor but this fact. Every poem bears the mark of its creator, as does each work of art you would gaze upon and call a masterpiece, as well as those creations of little hands you hang on refrigerator doors or office walls. You did not create yourself, and yet you make of life a re-creation of yourself and in so doing try to prove that you are your own source.

11.3   This is one reason you do not like the idea that those who would instruct you know more than you now know, and why you begin each new course of learning by feeling as if you have less. You then begin your attempts to acquire what you lack, so that you no longer have less than anyone else. Some of you may be confident in your learning skills and rush in to conquer this new territory as you have others that have come before. These would read each book as quickly as they can, with highlighter in tow, and when they have turned the last page be done with learning what this book would have to teach and rush on to the next. Those of you less confident may quit before you begin in order to keep from failing one more time. Even those who feel the power of these words within their hearts and vow to go slowly and carefully through each page and section, giving total dedication to what this text would have them do, are at risk of trying too hard to be earnest rather than simply desiring to learn.

11.4   Each one of these risks I have sought to limit by limiting the exercises to a simple few that will stay with you when all hurrying, fear of failing, and earnest attempts at trying hard have long been past. Each exercise is but an idea, and ideas leave not their source. All ideas here are but ideas of union come to replace ideas of separation. This will happen of its own without your understanding as long as you remain willing for the ideas to dwell within you, and you do not try to shut them out. Realize that the ideas of both success and failure are detrimental here. To feel you have achieved success in learning what love is all about is as ridiculous as feeling as if you have failed to learn what love is. Neither can happen. And your perception that either can will shut out all ideas of union.

What love is cannot be taught. Remember that your task   II.5
here is to remove the barriers that keep you from realizing what love is. That is the learning goal of this course — your awareness of what love is — and no earthly course can take you beyond this goal. It is only your willingness that is required.

Willingness must thus be talked about and separated from   II.6
what you would have it be. Willingness and faith go together. What you have faith in, you will see. This course asks for your willingness to have faith in something new. You have placed your faith in what you have made, and while it remains there you remain unwilling to relinquish illusion's hold on you. You can be faithful to but one thought system. One is the thought system of the separated self and is based on separation. The other is the thought system of creation and is based on union. Your faith in what you have made has been shaken now, and you realize you would like to place your faith elsewhere. You would like to, but you have your doubts, and this is where you become confused on the issue of willingness.

Willingness does not arise from conviction but brings con-   II.7
viction. Willingness is your declaration of openness, not necessarily of firm belief. You see free will and willingness together and while they are the same, their application is quite different.

11.8   Your free will you guard most closely, knowing this is what made the separation possible. You regard it as your one protection from God, the one thing that allows you to be other than what God would have you be. It is your "God given" right of independence, that which allowed you to leave God's side the way a child reaching the age of adulthood has the right to leave her parent's home.

11.9   To think you must protect anything from God is insane, and you know that this is so. But because you view free will as all you have that God cannot take away from you, you have not yet given up its protection. It does not matter to you that it is insane to think that He who has given you everything seeks to take anything away from you. While you still view yourself as a body, you cannot help but think of God as a vengeful God whose final vengeance is your own death. While you still think of your self as a body, it is easier to accept that your banishment from paradise was God's decision, not your own. You think you can be grateful to Him for some things and blame Him for others. Yes, perhaps this God you think you know has given you everything, but He can also take it all away, and in the end He surely will. He then will judge you and determine if you should be rewarded for a life of goodness or punished for a life of evil. He might accept you back, but He might not. A God such as this would seem to have little faith in you and to deserve little of your faith in return.

11.10   And so you give to God a little faith and cherish your free will, the true god of the separated self. You think at times that this was God's mistake, the one weakness in His plan, and one that you would use. At other times you think that this was but God's curse on you, a thing to tempt you to the life of desperation that you live. But your strongest perception of your free will is of its power. No matter what God wants of you, you can use your free will to rebel and to make your own choices, choices different than those your Creator would make for you. This right to make your own decisions, and the power to flaunt them before God, is all that makes your little separated self feel powerful at all.

You do not see that what you choose to do with your free 11.11 will matters not to God at all, for what you have chosen to use it for is the one thing that it cannot provide — your separation from your Creator. He remains as He is, as you remain as you are.

It is true that your free will is powerful as it is part, but only 11.12 part, of what has allowed you to believe in your separated state. While you could have used your free will to create like unto your Father, by choosing to make yourself separate from Him — something that could never truly occur — you have chosen instead to do nothing at all with your free will but make this one insane choice. Your willingness to make a new choice is what will once again make your free will like unto your Father's will, which is one with it in truth.

Your protectiveness of your free will is why we must sepa- 11.13 rate willingness from your perception of free will. Your free will is the last bastion of your separate army, the final line of defense, the site where the final battle will take place. Before this final battle is reached your willingness to change your mind about its need to be fought is what is desired by your Father and this Course.

God will never wrestle your free will from you, or fight 11.14 battles to win it for Himself. This final battle is in your own mind, and it is a figment of the illusions you have made. Let this prophecy you have made go, and realize that willingness does not negate free will. Yet even while you cannot yet quite give up your guardianship of it, it is sufficient to begin with a temporary choice, though a lasting choice will be required before you will feel the shift of cause and quit worrying about effect. For now what you desire are effects, without realizing cause must shift to change the effects you would have come about. This matters not at this point. You are offered the opportunity to make a temporary decision that can be rescinded at any time. Your temporary willingness will be enough to begin to effect cause and in doing so to bring some sanity to your restless mind and heart.

11.15   What willingness is it that you are asked to give? It can come in many manners and be given many forms. It can be called a willingness to change your mind, or to allow yourself to be open to new possibilities. It can be called a change of heart, or a willingness but to, for a little while, withdraw your fear and your protection from it. But what this willingness really does is allow your call to be sounded, your call to love and to be loved. It is a willingness to receive love from your Source and to be loved for who you are. Is this so much to ask?

11.16   It is a call that comes not from weakness but from strength, and that goes out to truth and not illusion. It is a call whose answer will come to you quickly on the wings of angels, a fluttering your heart will feel, for angels too are one with you. It may feel like loneliness compounded for the brief instant you await its coming and feel the emptiness that has been opened for its coming.

11.17   This is a call that requires you to do nothing but to remain faithful to it. You do not need to think about it, but only let it be. You need put no words on it, for words cannot express it any more than words can teach you what love is — or that love is. You need not concentrate on where to find love, for love will find you. You need not concentrate on giving love, for you cannot give what you do not yet know, and when you know it you need not give it, for it will extend from you naturally in miracles called love. Love is all that will fill your emptiness, and all that will never leave you empty again as it extends from you to your brothers and sisters. Love is all that will not leave you wanting. Love is all that will replace use with unity.

You exist, quite simply, because of your relationship with love. Love is the unity you seek. In having chosen separation over unity, you but chose fear over love. When you let go of fear and invite unity to return, you but send out an invitation to love and say *you are welcome here*. What is a dinner party where love is not? It is merely a social obligation. But a dinner party where love is welcomed to take its place becomes a celebration. Your table becomes an altar to the Lord and grace is upon it and the Lord is with you.

11.18

What we call Father is but creation's heavenly face, a personification of what cannot truly be personified. You find it hard to believe creation itself can be benevolent and kind, or just another name for love, but such it is. God is but creation's starting point, the creator of creation and yet creation itself. — 12.24

The word *love* is part of your problem with this Course. If I 12.1 were to take the word love and change it to some sophisticated-sounding technical term, and say this is the stuff that binds the world together in unity, it would be easier for you to accept. If I were to say you know not of this sophisticated term and this is why you have believed in your separation rather than in your unity with all things, you would be far more likely to nod your head and say, "I was but ignorant of this, as was everyone else." If a scientist was to tell you that a benign energy had been found that proved your connection to everything in the universe, and gave it some fancy name, you would say, "A new discovery has been found and I am willing to believe it may be true, especially if others are also going to believe it to be true."

You feel a little duped at being told love is the answer. You 12.2 feel a little chastised to be told you know love not. You feel a little deceived to think that love may not be limited to what you have thought it to be. You think it is typical of a spiritual text to tell you love is the answer, as if it has not been said before. This message was preached long ago and still the world remains the same. How could this be the correct answer when this is so? Life is too complicated to be solved by love.

12.3   How quickly you would return to cynicism and to believing you have already tried and failed. For all of you believe that you have tried this idea called love, and all of you believe you have evidence that it is not the answer at all. What is your evidence? Your own failure to be happy and the unhappiness of the world you see.

12.4   We have said before the only meaning possible for your free will is your choice of what to join with and your choice of what to leave outside of yourself. Yet you must understand that nothing that is not part of God is worthy of joining, nor *can* join with you. What you have sought to join with is the reason for your unhappiness. For you seek to join with what cannot be joined, and you seek separation from all that could be joined with you and all that would fill your dark and lonely places with the happiness you seek.

12.5   This Course may seem to have come far astray from what you would have it do, for you are looking for something specific from it, though you know it not. You are looking for the rest and quiet joy that only comes from love. You are looking for the safety and security of a loving home, even if it is one only of philosophy. You look for the soft assurance of certainty, not of your mind but of your heart. There is a part of you that thinks, *"If I could just be sure..."* and stops there, for you are not even sure of what it is you seek assurance. And yet you know what tires you most is your inability to be certain of anything. And you are tired indeed.

God's will for you is happiness, and of this you can be cer- 12.6
tain. To align your will with God's is but to make this certain state your home. This is but a wish come true, and
when it is all you wish for it will come to be. And in the
granting of this wish will come your rest and the laying
down of every heavy burden you have carried.

Admit now your desire to rest, a desire that could make you 12.7
weep and make you wish to sleep an endless sleep. If you but
understood the energy required to keep the world of your
illusion in its place, you would understand the rest that will
simply come of giving up your need to do so. Your desire
for certainty is part of your resistance to any ideas that seem
to be about change. What little that you think you know, you
would strive to keep, and yet deep down you realize that
you know nothing with the certainty you seek.

Uncertainty of any kind is doubt about your self. This is 12.8
why this Course aims to establish your identity, for from it
all the rest will come. As such, this Course seems to ask for
change at every level, and yet from one change alone will all
the others follow — and through no effort on your part at
all. And even this one change is not a change at all, for it
merely seeks to remove all the changes you but think that
you have made to God's creation. This change seeks but to
restore you to your Self.

Your Self rests totally unchanged within the Christ in you. 12.9
Reestablishing your relationship with your brother is what
will show your Self to you. You have one brother who wears
but many faces in your perception of who he is, and while
you know him not you cannot know your Self. This one
brother can unite you with all whom you perceive as others,
for all others are one with him as well as you. This is the one
joining that needs to occur to bring about all the rest.

12.10 This is the one disjoining that your choice for separation brought about, and it is but a separation from your Self. This is the most difficult point to get across, because in it lies a contradiction, the one contradiction that has created the world you see and the life you live. Although it is impossible for something to have gone wrong in God's creation, something has gone wrong! All you need do is look about you to know that this is so — and, rather than be discouraged by this news, you breathe a sigh of relief because you knew this to be true and yet have felt as if this is the secret that has been kept from you. It is as if you are told endlessly "everything is fine" while you know this is not true. And if "everything" is fine, it must just be you who are all wrong.

12.11 All of creation seems to hum along in perfect harmony. The stars light up the sky, the sun and moon do what they were appointed to do, the animals of the sea, ground, and air are but what their creator bade them be, the mountains stand in all their majesty, rivers flow and desert sands countless in number are blown endlessly about. Everything seems to be what it is and what it has always been, but for, perhaps, the mark of man upon it. Yet the moon remains the moon despite man's landing on it. The earth remains the earth despite your highways, roads, and bridges. And somewhere you know not, peace remains peace despite your wars, and happiness remains happiness despite your despair.

12.12 Yet what of you? You, too, seem to have remained the same for countless ages. Perhaps you believe that long ago you evolved from a form different than that which you inhabit now; but certainly within the laws of evolution, you have changed as little as the birds of the air or fish of the sea. Yet somehow you know that in all of creation, it is humanity alone that somehow is not what it was meant to be. On a lovely day and in a lovely place you can see that creation's paradise still exists, but nowhere can you find the being God created in His image.

Does it make any sense at all that this would come to be? Or that once upon a time there walked upon the earth those who did reveal God's image, and that when they ceased to be seen here God's image was lost to earth forever? Could even one have come and gone and left this void forever more unfilled? A gaping hole within the universe itself? 12.13

But one was needed to end the separation, and in this one are all the rest joined. For what alone in all creation could be affected by your free will but your own self? But one was needed to, of his own free will, join his will with his Father's for it to be done for all. This is all correction or atonement means, and all that is in need of your acceptance. Join your brother who made this choice for all, and you are reunited with the Christ in you. 12.14

Joined minds cannot think separately and have no hidden thoughts. They are, in fact, not minds in the plural at all, but all-one-mind. What this Course is saying is that at some point that does not exist in time, God's son made the choice for separation. Whether God's son had one form or many at that time matters not, for one form or many, there was still one mind, the mind of God's son joined in unity with that of his Father. Many of you have been taught this mystery of faith. Father, Son, and Holy Spirit are One. If you had indeed learned what you were taught, the separation would be no more. 12.15

These words, *Father, Son,* and *Holy Spirit,* like the word *love,* are but symbols representing ideas that represent what is. That you have made of the Father a singular figure, some-how greater than the Son, and accepted the Holy Spirit as 12.16

something largely not within your understanding, only exemplifies the nature of the error in need of correction. While words, as symbols, cannot fully explain what cannot be symbolized, a beginning is made that must be completed through the memories of your heart. So we continue, realizing that these words can express the truth only within their ability as symbols, and that farther than where these symbols can take you, the truth lies within yourself.

12.17 You have all seen the way a thought that seems to arise out of nowhere can affect you. An idea, birthed one day, does not seem to have been there the day before. Perhaps it is the idea of taking a trip or having a baby, of returning to school, or quitting a job. This idea, newly birthed, may seem to come and go, or may grow into an obsession, but either way, it leaves not its source. And without the birth of the idea, the results of the idea would not come to be. You may have a thousand ideas one day and ten thousand the next, so many that you could never keep track of them all, and yet they still exist within you and do not splinter off and become something on their own apart from you. Imagine this occurring and you will see how senseless this situation would be. Could a trip happen on its own? To whom would it happen?

12.18 You may very well say, however, that an idea seemed to take on a life of its own and compel you to do things you might have never dreamed of doing. People often look back upon their lives and wonder how they got from here to there, and some may see that one idea took root and changed what seemed to be a destiny already written.

12.19 As near as words can describe the separation, this is what occurred: An idea of separation entered the mind of God's son. Like any idea of yours, this idea did not leave its source nor change the essence of its source in any way. While the idea of taking an adventurous vacation when brought to fruition might reshape the life of the one participating in it, it would not change who that person was, or who his father was, or the nature of the family he was born into. All that would change would be the shape of his life, the things that would happen within it, perhaps the places in which it would occur or the people that would be part of it. In short, the external aspects of the life.

From the idea of separation came the idea of an external aspect of life. Before the idea of the separation, there was no such thing — and there still is no such thing except as an extension of the original idea. Just as we discussed your desire to protect or to control proceeding from the concept of fear, and realized that without fear they would not exist, so, too, is it with the external aspect of life. Without the original idea of separation, the external aspect of life would not exist. Just as fear is not real although it seems to be, separation is not real although it seems to be. 12.20

The Father did not prevent the idea of separation from taking place, and could not any more than you could prevent an idea from occurring to you. Just as an idea of yours, once born, continues to exist, so, too, does this idea of separation. But just as your ideas do not take on a life of their own even though they at times seem to, this idea as well had no ability to be more than what it was, *except for* as the son chose to participate in it. 12.21

Thus, the son's participation in the idea of separation seemed to bring about a completely reshaped life, a destiny different than that which had already been written. Yet this participation could not but proceed from the original idea and could not proceed in reality but only in the external aspect of life that preceded it. The idea of separation 12.22

changed nothing in reality, but became a drama acted out upon a stage so real that it seemed to be reality.

12.23 Separation is painful only to those who believe it can occur in truth. What would a child's rejection or a parent's death mean to those who did not believe in separation? Do you believe that God believes in separation? He knows it not, and because He knows it not, it does not exist. Because He knows it not, He has not been hurt by it. He knows no rejection and no death. He knows no pain or sorrow. His son remains with Him in his eternal home, joined with Him as always in eternal completion.

12.24 Yet while the son's extension into an external world is quite real, it is all that is truly real within it. The son could not create unlike the Father who created everything by extension of Himself. Neither the Father's extension, nor the Son's, lessened Father or Son in any way. Replace the word Father with the word Creation and see if this does not help to make this concept clear. Could creation's continuing extension of itself, its continuing creation, make less of it than what it started out to be? What we call Father is but creation's heavenly face, a personification of what cannot truly be personified. You find it hard to believe creation itself can be benevolent and kind, or just another name for love, but such it is. God is but creation's starting point, the creator of creation and yet creation itself. The Son and Holy Spirit, like unto creation, proceeded from the starting point of God. God is the Son and Holy Spirit's starting point as well, the creator of the Son and Holy Spirit, yet He also is the Son and Holy Spirit.

12.25 Now, carry this pattern forward, for the pattern of God's extension is the pattern of creation and thus the pattern of the universe. The Son extended himself into creation, and you are that extension and as holy as he is. The idea of separation only seems to have made God's son susceptible to division, and these word symbols are all that seem to separate Father, Son, and Holy Spirit from creation or from each other.

𝒲hile you will not realize it at first, because you have no experience but only memory of feeling yourself in such a way, you will eventually realize that the memories you recall of the spirit of others include memories that are your own, memories that are of your own Self. For no spirit exists that is not part of you, or you of it. — 13.8

You will never fully "understand" what unity means, but you *will* come to feel what unity means, and this I promise you. This is what we work toward in this Course, for once you have experienced the feeling of unity, you will need no understanding of it. This is all the exercises that call you to observe your body are for. They are the preparation for what is to come: the preparation for feeling that which is not of your body. Our next exercise takes this one step further, and is merely an extension of the first. In this exercise you will begin to realize that your brothers and sisters are not their bodies, anymore than you are yours. This is a natural extension of observing your body in action, because as your body seems to interact with others and as you observe this interaction, you will "see" yourself and others in a new light. Your body will seem more connected with those of the others it interacts with, for they will be grouped together in your observation of them. It will not be only others you observe but yourself and others, placing you and "them" together where you belong. This seeming togetherness of bodies is just a first step that will take you beyond the illusion of bodies to togetherness of spirit.

13.1

13.2 As you observe, always with your heart and not your mind, and begin to include others in your observation, I ask you to concentrate on one thing only. This is a simple exercise, and enjoyable too. It but calls for you to ask one thing: Ask yourself what you already know of the spirit of the person you observe. You will be amazed at the knowledge you already have and the joy it brings you to remember it.

13.3 These are but exercises in memory recollection, and the more you practice them the more true memory will return to you. Do not apply any effort to these exercises, particularly not that of recalling spirit. Just let impressions come to you, and when they make you feel like smiling know that you are feeling memory return. If, when trying to call up memory of spirit, you find your brow knitting in concentration, you are applying effort and need to cease attempting the exercise at that time. If you give this exercise just the tiniest bit of consistent practice, however, it will soon become routine to you, for you will want to continuously experience the pleasure that it brings.

13.4 While you may desire to put what you feel into words, this exercise is not about putting words on feelings or using them to describe spirit. It is best to leave words off this experience as, if you do not, you will soon be ascribing some attributes to one spirit and not to another, just to differentiate between them. The purpose here is to show you that they cannot be differentiated or compared or defined in the same way you have defined their bodies in the past.

13.5 You will soon find that what you recall of spirit is love. You will want to give it many names at first, and might not even recognize it as love, for it will come without all the longing and sadness you so often associate with it. While the feeling of love that washes over you from one may feel like courage, and from another like gentleness, and while this is all part of what you are encouraged to feel, it is simply asked that you let the feelings come and with them the realization that while no two spirits will seem exactly the same, they also are not "different." The love from each will fill you with happiness because it is already complete and has no needs and so no sense of longing or sadness of any kind. Because it is complete, it will ask nothing of you, but will seem to offer you a warm welcome, as if you are a long lost friend returning home.

And so you are. This is the new "proof" that, while not sci- 13.6 entific or verifiable, will offer you the evidence you seek to confirm the truth of what you are being told here. All that is required to gather this new evidence is to trust in your own heart. Are you willing to believe what your heart would tell you?

This exercise should take no time nor break your stride or 13.7 the flow of your conversation. All it asks you to do is to become aware of spirit and to allow this awareness to abide within you. If you feel resistance to attempting this exercise, remember that you already know that you are more than your body, and ask yourself if it makes sense to not do all you can to become aware of the "more" you know you are.

While you will not realize it at first, because you have no 13.8 experience but only memory of feeling yourself in such a way, you will eventually realize that the memories you recall of the spirit of others include memories that are your own, memories that are of your own Self. For no spirit exists that is not part of you, or you of it. If you find yourself distracted by these memories, do not push them aside as interruptions in your day, but know that anything that distracts you from the little self you think you are is worth the minutes you would give to its contemplation.

13.9   What further objections can you have? Here we ask you not to follow any instruction other than that of your own Self. We invite the return of what you know, and let your real Self guide you gently back to where you want to be and already are in truth.

13.10   Your ego will strongly resist your attempts to listen to your heart, and will call this every kind of foolishness, a waste of time that could be spent on better things. Yet time is not required, nor is money or the use of any other thing you value. And there is not even the slightest chance of being made to look foolish by what you are asked to do.

13.11   Might some of your preconceived notions of others and yourself be shattered? Oh yes, and rightly so. Gladly will you let them go and, if you trust yourself, all the evidence against your brother that you have stored up in your lifetime will be let go as well.

13.12   Each of you will initially find it difficult to accept the innocence and sinlessness of others and yourself, for your memory will contain no hint of past misdeeds, errors, or mistakes. No one will have leveled any hurts on you or anyone else. No reason for guilt will exist within this memory. No shame or fear is here, and no grievances of any kind. For here forgiveness is already accomplished — and when memory of forgiveness returns to you, can memory of your Father or your own Self be far behind?

14 | SPECIAL RELATIONSHIPS EARTHLY and HUMAN

It is your response to love that concerns us now, for the return of love is coming and you do not want to make the same response again.

— 14.14

The purpose of the life you share here with your brothers and your sisters has been to challenge God's creation. Now your united purpose must change to that of remembering who you are *within* God's creation, rather than in the world that you have made. Think but a minute of this, and you will begin to see the enormity of the difference in these two purposes. 14.1

Is it not true that you have made an enemy of creation? Do you feel part of it and at one with all within it? If not, you have made yourself creation's enemy. You seek to be different from all the rest, and in this seeking proclaim that one part of creation is better than another part. You thus seek to fragment creation as you have fragmented your own self. And from the vantage point you have established in which you view yourself as the epitome of God's creation, you see the rest of creation as being meant to serve your ends. And since your *end* or goal is that of separation and being different from all the rest, this is the goal you ask creation to bow down to, a goal that never can be achieved any 14.2

more than can your separation from what you think is unlike you.

14.3 You cannot have feelings of superiority and not an enemy make. The same occurs when you would make yourself inferior, and you are always making for yourself a place at one of these extremes. And all this effort and conflict arises simply from your insistence upon being separate. He who is your enemy you cannot help but be at war with. Where there is war there can be no peace. War is not simply the existence of external activity. External activity is but the effect of a cause that remains internal, and all war is but war upon yourself.

14.4 Do you not see how your notion of heaven being an attainment you can reach only after death fits your goal of separation? If your belief in heaven were true, your challenge to creation would be real and only your death would prove the victor. For if after death your creator God provided you with a paradise not of this world, a separate place to honor your specialness and separation from all else that He created, then would you be vindicated and the purpose of your war made holy. You would be proven right and creation wrong.

14.5 Would this make sense? What creator would create a world in which the highest achievement of the life upon it would be to leave it in order to gain life? What creator would create a world not meant to exist in harmony? Harmony is life. What creator would create a temporary life and hold eternal life as a reward for death?

14.6 If you can see the senselessness of a creator and a creation such as this and still believe in it, then you must believe in a god who is insane. You, who pride yourself on reason and practicality: think if a creation such as this could contain any reason whatsoever. Why then do you believe in it?

You who have made a god of reason and of intellect, think 14.7
carefully now of what your reason and your intellect have made for you. How terrible would it really be to realize that although you have tried mightily, a creation such as this cannot be made to make any sense at all? Those who have turned their backs on God and refused to believe in such nonsense have simply refused to make reason try to fit the unfitable without seeing that an alternative exists.

You are not asked to believe the unbelievable, or to disregard 14.8
all that reason would say to you. Only the opposite is true. You are asked rather to give up the laws of chaos for the laws of reason. The laws of illusion for the laws of truth.

Think you not that reason opposes love, for love gives rea- 14.9
son its foundation. The foundation of your insane world is fear. The foundation of Heaven, your true home, is love. The same world based upon these different foundations could not help but look quite different.

Your ideas of love, however, fit your goal of separation as 14.10
neatly and conveniently as does your idea of heaven. For what you require of love is that it set you apart and make you special. Much more is demanded of those you love than of any of your other brothers and sisters. The *more* that is required is all to feed your idea of your own specialness. You look for constant verification that this one you love loves you in return, and if this attention is not provided you feel you have cause for claiming wounds that cannot be healed and reparations that cannot be paid. You thus hold the one you love the most in the greatest bondage, and call that bondage a relationship.

14.11   This can be most clearly seen in relationships that were once "everything" to you and have since failed you. This can be a memory of any relationship, and each of you has one. It can be of parent and child, of best friends, of a marriage or a partnership, or even that of a mentor or student. Whatever the relationship's configuration, it was one that truly brought you joy. Within it you were happy and felt as if you needed nothing more than this. It was a relationship so intense that at its peak you would have begun to see its continuation without change as the major goal of your life. Without it, life would not be worth living, and so it was necessary to retain it at all cost.

14.12   This is a classic example that reveals much to you about yourself and the world you have made if you are but willing to look at it with eyes that truly see. It is the magnifying glass that will allow you to see your world in all its mad confusion. For what caused you such great joy seemed to come at the cost of pain and to leave you more alone and comfortless than before. How could this be said of love? And how could it have failed you so? And how, if it were real — as it surely felt as if it was — could it prove anything but that love is no answer, and surely not for you?

14.13   We must begin with what is obvious, a simple point that some of you have denied and that some of you could not. What makes this relationship stand out in your mind and feel so painful in your memory of it is that it was quite real in a way that is different from your relationships before or since. No other relationship affected you in such a way. Never were you more sure of a relationship's value to you. Anything that could make you feel so joyous, so safe and warm and loved, could not help but hold a value quite beyond compare. In this you were correct. It was no illusion that caused you to feel this way. This was not the love that passes for love in this world, but something else entirely. For at least one brief moment, this was true love, for nothing but love can be the cause of joy, nor offer a haven of safety in an insane world.

It is your response to love that concerns us now, for the return of love is coming and you do not want to make the same response again.   14.14

Everything that you consider valuable you want to keep. This makes perfect sense to you because the foundation of your world is fear. Were the foundation of your world love, everything that you consider valuable you could not wait to share. Perhaps you think the desire to keep things for yourself stems from something other than fear. You might call this desire pride or security, or even accept that it is vanity, before you would call it fear. But fear is what it is.   14.15

Only fear breeds the feelings of lack that stand with it, the cornerstone of the foundation of your separate world. You do not realize that you have created a universe for yourself, a universe that you are required to maintain, and that without your effort would dissolve. This universe is yourself and you are everything in it. Do you not believe that were you to perish something quite unique would be lost to the world? You are alone and irreplaceable: one of a kind. Within you lie all that you would hope to contribute and create. Within the actions and interactions of your lifetime lie all the effects you would hope to have on what remains here. Without you, the people and the events that you would influence, would behave quite differently and bring about different results than are somehow meant to occur. Although you know not your purpose, at least a part of you believes that this is true, for there must be some reason for your existence — although you cannot quite imagine what   14.16

that reason might be. You must be meant to be because you *are,* and you cannot fathom that you would exist at all if there were not a reason for you to do so.

14.17   Is this not a description of a universe? What is a universe but itself and everything in it? Nothing would seem to exist outside of it, and so it must be unique. Everything that would happen within the universe would depend upon it.

14.18   You think that you are quite aware of your small space within the universe, and that it is foolishness to say that you think otherwise. Yet, since only what you know is part of your universe, do you not see that it depends on you, and if it depends on you that it is you? Only what you are aware of exists in the universe that is you. Only what happens to you affects your universe. Your universe is completely different than anyone else's and completely self-contained. The laws of your universe are for the maintenance of your body, because without it you would not exist. And when you cease to exist, so does your universe. The lights will be turned out upon it and it will be no more.

14.19   What a big job you have assigned yourself! It is no small wonder that you live in fear when so much is dependent upon you. And no wonder that when you find a respite, a place of rest and beauty and of love, you want to claim it for your own lest it get away! It too must be maintained within your universe, or you will know it not and its benefits will escape and be lost to you. You wish that you could join with it and make it one with you, but since you know not that this can be done or how to do it, you try to accomplish the "next best thing" and keep it close to you, a twin universe still existing separately, but close enough that you can gaze upon it and feel the benefit of its warmth because of its proximity. More than this you cannot do, but still you try. With chains you would bind this separate universe to your own, for as long as it maintains its autonomy, which it must, even its nearness is not enough. And so what you attempt next is an exchange of sorts. Like two countries, one rich in oil, another in grain, you set up dependencies that will keep you linked. Some of you do this quite obviously, and over years and years create a web of intricate design, a snare or trap that seems impossible to dismantle because of its interconnections. Others experience this plan of entrapment solely in their mind as they plot and plan for what they never have the opportunity to put into place. Still others are more coy in their design, and dress it up to look like sacrifice and gifts given, but all with the same purpose in mind. What none realize is that fear has replaced love.

Some may realize that they are afraid of losing love, and even 14.20 speak of it and try to alleviate the fear with official commitments, pledges, and promises made. Others may deny their fear, and say they trust in what they have and the faithfulness of the one they love. Fewer than these are those who do not need to voice their faith and trust, for their feelings remain strong despite their fear. For even those who fear no deception must remain afraid of the great deceiver. Whether they call it life or death, it is still the same. It is the chance that cannot be foreseen but is always there: death may take their loved one prematurely, and if not prematurely certainly eventually.

And all of these, those who would admit to fear, and those 14.21 who won't, would still believe that love exists despite fear's claim upon it, and think that they are lucky to have found a love to shield them for a little while from all the other things they fear. And yet the greatest fear of all is that of loss of love. You who have given everything to be alone and separate fear most of all that which you have given everything to attain.

For what is loss of love but confirmation of your separate state? What is loss of love but being left alone?

14.22   Loss of love comes from only one source. Call it fear or call it separation but it is still the same. For in your separated state you ask that love make you special to someone else, and that one special to you. You think this is what love is for, and so you make of it something it is not and only call it love.

14.23   Heaven can only be made to seem to fit your goal of separation, and the same is true of love. You cannot change what love is or what heaven is. All that seems to make it change is the function or purpose you would give it. It is but you who gave heaven the purpose of giving you something to look forward to, a reward for a life lived according to your own rules, a reward to be gained by some and not by others, a pinnacle of achievement that will prove your rightness and your success after you are gone. Love you give the same purpose, but bid it do the job of rewarding you here and now. It, like heaven, is your proof that you are good and worthy, special and to be rewarded for your specialness.

14.24   You have thus placed love and heaven together in a parody of creation's meaning of each. Yes, they go together, and this you know; but the purpose of neither is what you have ascribed it to be. The purpose you give each thing within your world is what makes it what it is to you. And as each purpose you have ascribed to anything proceeds from the foundation of fear that built your world, each purpose is as senseless and as reversed from the truth as is the next.

14.25   This is why this Course cannot just talk of love and bring you any closer to it than you are. While you realize not the purpose of anything in truth, you cannot know love or your own Self.

While your purpose remains to make yourself and others special, you will not put an end to the separation. And you cannot just let go of your own specialness. For as long as you hold on to the specialness of others you hold on to your own. There is no reason to hold on to another's specialness unless you hold on to your own. And what you give to others you keep for yourself. Give another specialness, and you keep it for yourself as well as see it in them instead of seeing their glory. Specialness keeps them separate, and therefore susceptible to loss. How can you lose what is one with you? You cannot. You can only lose that which is separate. And specialness does make separate.

14.26

This is the problem compounded in your "special" love relationships of having experienced real specialness, which is not specialness at all but glory. Your joining caused this, for each joining brings you in touch with your brother. Each joining returns you to your holy relationship with your brother, which is the only one you have in truth. Only this relationship is real, and in it are included all others. One does not discard or replace the other. What is real is all-inclusive. What is unreal is nothing.

14.27

You who do not know how to trade your separated state for that of union have still done so when you have loved freely and without fear. In this state your memory returns to you of who you are, and you are innocent and joyous and one with love itself. That this memory does not last, and these feelings seem unsustainable, is the result only of that which does discard and replace. As we have said before, there are but two emotions. One is love, the other fear. Fear, through your own choice, replaces and discards love. Fear is always strongest when you value something that you feel may be threatened. Love threatens most your specialness. Before your conscious mind has any awareness of what is

14.28

happening, your memory of love, of innocence and of joy, threatens your specialness, your ego, your separated self, who quickly rushes in with love's replacement. Nothing but fear could take the memory of love from you, or replace so quickly the glory that is your nature with the specialness that is not.

14.29   You think love is what you value most, and so resist any notion that what you view as love is not what you think it is. But as long as you equate love with the special ones on whom you choose to bestow it, you will know love not. What you will know is specialness, raised to the level of the Almighty and set upon His throne in a crown of jewels.

14.30   In your world love has no meaning unless it is attached to a particular thing. And as soon as love is attached to a particular, love's opposite is brought into existence. While you refuse to look upon this simple fact, you have no hope of change, nor does your world. You who think, *"What harm can come of loving this one above all others?"* think again. For you are choosing not to love but to make special. And you are choosing but to make love's opposite real to you and those you claim to love, as well as those you claim not to love.

14.31   Let us ask instead how loving all as one can bring harm? If you love all the same, what loss is there to anyone, including the one you would choose to make special? All that is lost is specialness. This is the view of life you cannot imagine bringing about, or bringing joy in its coming. But this is what you must begin to imagine if you desire to accept love's coming instead of to reject it once again. For your refusal to give up specialness is your refusal of the Christ in you and a refusal of love itself.

What harm is there in specialness? Only all the harm you see within the world.

— 15.2

We have talked much now of your special love for others, 15.1
but what of the specialness you desire for yourself? Do you
not see how intricately linked these two desires are? The
desire to give and receive specialness is the driving desire of
your life, and the world you see but reflects this desire.
Love's opposite would not exist but for your invitation of it.
All hate, guilt, shame, and envy are but the result of your
creation of an opposite to love through specialness. All the
maladies of the current time as well as those of history
would give way to love without the interference of all
that would make special. You think issues of survival rule the
world — and so they do, but they would not if it were not
for your need to be special. Transportation would be transportation rather than a status symbol. Without a desire
for specialness, a person would have no need for status at all.
Beauty would be what it is and not what products
would make it. Without a desire for specialness, a person
would have no need for products at all. Wealth would be the
happy state of everyone, for without specialness to feed,
there would be neither want nor hunger. Without a desire

for specialness there would be no war, for there would be no reason to break the peace. No land would be considered more sacred to some than others, no resources withheld, no people deemed subservient.

15.2   What harm is there in specialness? Only all the harm you see within the world.

15.3   While you desire specialness for yourself, your true Self will remain hidden and unknown, and since this is a Course that seeks to reveal your true identity, specialness must be seen for what it is so that you will desire it no longer. You can have specialness or your true Self, but never both. The desire for specialness is what calls your little self into being. This is the self that is easily wounded, the self that takes on grievances and refuses to give them up, the self that is prone to pettiness and bitterness, resentment and deception. Be truthful as you examine yourself and you will see that this is so.

15.4   It is more difficult to see that this desire for specialness does not stop with what would bring misery to your own mind and heart. Perhaps the leader of some impoverished country brings misery to others with his desire for specialness, but not you. Yes, taken on a grand scale, you can see that this desire can wreak havoc; but still you would not believe that your own desire for specialness or to make another special could make a difference to many — or possibly even to anyone. You just want to love your mate and children, your parents or your friends, and would be quite content to have them think you special and to make them special to you. Out in the wider world you think you are anonymous and so are they. If within the small sphere of those they love they cannot be made to feel special — and you along with them — then what is the point of being here at all? For this is indeed the point you have made of your life.

And so within this small sphere you do what is necessary to   15.5
maintain your specialness and that of the others within it.
Depending on your culture, what is necessary may mean few
things, or many and different things for each one. From this
sphere of influence comes your notions of success, your ideas
of what is necessary to be good, your notions of what it
means to treat others well. You would not be special to this
one if you did not look a certain way, and you would not be
special to that one if you did not earn a certain amount of
money. You would not be special if you did not give this one
certain gifts and opportunities, nor would you fulfill your
responsibility of making this one special if you did not do so.
To make one small change in this culture is difficult to
impossible, because if you were to go your own way and
choose your own look, lifestyle, or attitude, you might risk
being seen as special within this group, and your choices
might affect your ability to make others feel special in the way
in which they have become accustomed to your doing so.

How many rest within this sphere of influence? Twenty, fifty,   15.6
one hundred? And how many times is this multiplied by
each of them? And yet this is but a fraction of whom your
specialness influences. In truth, your specialness affects
everyone.

Your desire for specialness makes of you a slave to others and   15.7
others to you. It diminishes your freedom, and for no end.
For what others think of you does not make you special, nor
does what you think or do for others make them special. All
notions of popularity, success, and competition begin here.
All notions of loyalty as well.

For now we come upon a linchpin in your plan for special-   15.8
ness — one of great necessity to overcome if you are to reach
the learning goal this Course has set. Loyalty stems from

faith, and where you set your faith is as much a determiner of your perception as is your concept of separation. All change seems to question your loyalty to others and all choices are made with this loyalty in mind. Loyalty stems here from your faith in fear and all from which you need protection. To belong to a loyal group, a family or community of supporters, is seen as necessary for your safety. While many of you do not have this, you strive for it, and its attainment has been the cause of much suffering in your world. This banding together for support against fear simply makes fear real, and the seeming cause for loyalty essential.

15.9   Your concept of loyalty is what makes it difficult for you to entertain withdrawing your effort to manifest the specialness of others and yourself. "Making special" seems to be a responsibility you have undertaken, and a refusal to make special an act of disloyalty. What's more, when all is said and done, you are loyal not only to your group but to humanity itself. Despite the many ills that have made you and those you love suffer, to call into question humanity's right to specialness seems the ultimate act of disloyalty to your own kind. To even think that you could change and be unlike others of your kind, you would call an act of treachery. To give your allegiance to your Father and to the learning goals this Course has set is but an act of treason upon the world as you know it.

15.10 And so it is. And so must your faith and loyalty be placed in something new, something worthy of your diligence and something that will not leave behind your brothers and your sisters to a life of suffering and of sin.

15.11 All suffering and sin come from specialness, and so it is but specialness you must leave behind. And there is a way to do so, a way that will not harm any of those you love even while betraying all they would hold dear. But which would you rather betray? The truth or illusion? You cannot be loyal to both, and herein lies your problem. For at the turning point you look back and see one other you cannot betray, and one other whose special treatment of yourself you cannot live without or abandon hope of receiving. And so you choose illusion over truth and betray all that you are and the hope your brother has placed in you as savior of the world.

You who still fantasize that you can have it both ways, give up your fantasy and realize that real choice lies before you. No, this is not an easy choice, or it would have been chosen long ago and saved much suffering and put an end to hell. But it also is not a difficult choice, nor one that is in truth yours alone to make. This choice cannot be made without your brother and is indeed your brother's holy choice, as well as his birthright and your own. You only need be open to the place that no specialness can enter, and bid your brother choose for you. For in his choice you join with him and with your Father. In this choice lies one united will for glory that knows neither specialness nor separation. In this choice lies life eternal.

15.12

CHAPTER 16

WHAT YOU
CHOOSE INSTEAD

$\mathcal{P}$ower is possessed by those who claim it. By those who cry I am. For the beginning of power comes from the rejection of powerlessness. The rejection of powerlessness is but a step toward your identity achieved through the awakening of love of self.
— 16.21

The glory that you felt from love only seemed to be available from one and not from another. Love is not available *from* anyone in the way you think it is. Love has but one Source! That this Source lies within each of you does not make it many sources, for the many of you have but one Source as well. This common Source does not make any of you special, but all of you the same.   16.1

You may ask now why it doesn't seem so, and the only answer is that you do not want it to. You perceive but what you wish for, and your wish for specialness leads you not to see sameness anywhere at all, for what is the same cannot be special.   16.2

You all are familiar with the "problem" child who seeks love and attention in ways deemed inappropriate. You know this child is no less than any other child, and what he seeks the same as any other. Yet if this child grows up with behavior that remains unchanged you call him deviant or criminal, and claim that it is not love he seeks, and that he is now less   16.3

than those who once were the same as he. What is the same does not change and become different. Innocence is not replaced by sin.

16.4   What you do to criminals you do but to yourself and to those you claim to love with a special love. For you do not see them in the changeless innocence in which they were created and remain, but with the eyes of judgment. That you have judged and found the ones you love good and worthy of your love makes not your judgment justified any more than the judgment that condemns a body to death or to "life" in prison.

16.5   Life in prison and a body condemned to death is what judgment does to all of you who believe that what is the same can be made different. This is as true of the love you reserve for special ones as it is of the condemnation you reserve for others you have singled out. For judgment is what is required to make one special and another not.

16.6   Without judgment there would be no separation, for you would see no difference between yourself and your brothers and sisters. Your judgment began with your own self, and from it was all conflict born. Without differences there is no cause for conflict. Judgment makes different. It looks past what is the same and sees it not and sees instead what it is looking for. What you are looking for is what you will find, but finding it does not make it the truth, except as it is the truth about what you choose to see. Your choice lies with God or with the self you believe you have succeeded in separating from Him, and based on this choice alone is how you see determined.

16.7   Judgment is the function the separated mind has given itself. This is where all of its energy is expended, for constant judgment is required to maintain the world you see. The Holy Spirit can replace your specialness with a special function; but this function cannot be yours while you choose judgment itself as your proper role.

Only your heart can lead you to the forgiveness that must overcome judgment. A forgiven world is a world whose foundation has changed from fear to love. Only from this world can your special function be fulfilled and bring the light to those who still live in darkness. 16.8

Child of God, see you how important it is that you listen to your heart! Your heart does not want to see with judgment or with fear. It calls to you to accept forgiveness that you may give it and henceforth look upon the forgiven world with love. 16.9

I repeat again that reason does not oppose love, as your split mind would have you believe it does. For your split mind judges even love and opposes it on the basis that it uses no judgment! Here you can see the value that you place on judgment, even to the ridiculous notion that you can judge judgment itself. You deem yourself capable of making good judgments and poor judgments, and you deem love as being capable of neither. Love seems to operate on its own apart from what your mind would bid it do, and this is why you fear it even while you yearn for it. This is what the split mind would call reason — a world in which there are two sides to everything and two sides that oppose each other. How can this be reason? The truth opposes nothing, nor does love. 16.10

Again your memory of creation serves you, even if it has not served you well. It is this memory that tells you that love does not judge, and only your split mind that has made of this memory what will serve its purpose. What it calls a 16.11

deficiency is your saving grace. Letting go of what your mind would tell you in favor of what your heart already knows is but the purpose of this Course.

16.12   Only forgiveness replaces judgment, but true forgiveness is as foreign to you as is true love. You think forgiveness looks upon another in judgment and pardons the wrongs you would enumerate. True forgiveness simply looks past illusion to the truth where there are no sins to be forgiven, no wrongs to be pardoned. Forgiveness looks on innocence and sees it where judgment would see it not.

16.13   This form of forgiveness seems impossible to you because you look upon an unforgiven world where evil walks, danger lurks, and nowhere is safety to be found. Each separated one is out for his or her own self, and if you do not watch out for your own safety, surely you will perish. Yet while you watch vigilantly you know that you cannot protect yourself and that you are not safe. There is only one of you and so many of "them." Never can you keep your guard up quite enough or secure a final guarantee against disaster. And yet you cling to all attempts to do so even while knowing they are ineffective.

16.14   You think you cannot give up your vigilance because you know no other way to ensure your safety, and even if you cannot guarantee your safety against everything all of the time, you believe you can guarantee your safety against some things some of the time. And for this occasional protection that has no validity and no proof you give up love!

16.15   While you claim you need proof before you can believe or accept something as a fact or as the truth, and certainly before you can act upon it, you live as if you believe that what has never worked before will somehow miraculously work in the future. You have nothing but evidence of a life of unhappiness and despair, where occasional moments of joy or the few people that you love out of the many that you do not are all that make your life worth living. You think that to be asked to give up the caution, protection, and vigilance that protects these moments of joy and people you love as well as your own self is to be asked to live a life of even greater risk than that which you live now.

Your judgment has not made the world a better place! If history proves anything, it proves the opposite of what you would care to believe. The more the individual, society, and culture indulge in the desire to judge, the more godlike they think they make themselves. For all of you here know that judgment is not your place, and that it belongs to God and God alone. This is firmly attached to your memory of creation. To wrestle the right to judge away from God is an act against God, and like a child who has dared to defy his parents, the act of defiance fills the defiant one with boldness. Something dangerous has been tried and has seemingly succeeded. The order of the universe has flipped. The child believes she has "stolen" the role of parent away from the parent without having become a parent. God has become the enemy to those who judge just as the parent of a defiant child becomes the enemy in the child's perception. 16.16

But the child is wrong. The child has made a mistake. And with this mistake, the child believes that the relationship with the parent has been severed. It is this belief in a severed relationship with God that seems to replace the holy relationship that cannot be replaced. Judgment thus reinforces the idea of separation, making of it something even darker than it started out as being. It no longer seems like a choice that the child has made, but seems to be an irreparable rift that a new choice cannot mend. 16.17

16.18   Child of God, this is not so and cannot ever be, for the right
to judge is but the right of the creator who judges all of creation as it was created and remains. You only think that you
have changed the unchangeable.

16.19   Judgment does not make you safe, and defining evil does
not abolish it, but only makes it real to you. Yet you believe
judgment to be based on justice, and justice to include the
punishment of those you have defined as evil. You have thus
made justice one with vengeance, and in doing so have
robbed justice of its meaning.

16.20   Those who sit in judgment call upon their power to do what
it cannot do. All power comes from love, as does all justice.
Any basis other than love for power or for justice makes a
mockery of both. *Might makes right* is a saying that is known
to many of you, and even those who know not the saying
believe in the tenets it represents. This, you will claim, you
have evidence for. It is all around you. The strong survive
and the weak perish. The mighty prevail, and so define
what is right for all those whom they prevail over. Those in
power are those who make the laws, and those who have
no power must obey them.

16.21   And yet you are as frightened of those who have no power
as those who do. Criminals are feared and shunned, and yet
they have no power but that which they make from their
own selves. You want power to come only through legiti-
mate channels and do not want those who have no power to
possess it through the same weapons or might that you claim
make those in authority powerful. While you want those
you have given power to protect you, you also fear them,
and they in turn fear the powerless who might take away
their power or rise up against them. What kind of power is
it that needs to be constantly defended? What is it about the

powerless that frightens you, except that they might not accept their powerless state? And what does this say but what history has shown you — that who is powerful and who is not is not determined by might or any authority that can be given and taken away. Power is possessed by those who claim it. By those who cry *I am.* For the beginning of power comes from the rejection of powerlessness. The rejection of power- lessness is but a step toward your identity achieved through the awakening of love of Self.

What misery the world has suffered in the name of judg- 16.22 ment, power, and justice. What misery can be avoided by finding the true power inherent in your identity. For you are not powerless. Yet those of you who think you have tradi- tional means of power on your side turn not to your own power, and then you wonder why those most spiritual, both currently and historically, seem to suffer hardship. Yet it is often only those who suffer hardship who will rise up and claim the power that is their own instead of looking for it elsewhere. Your perception but looks at power backwards and wonders why God has forsaken a people who seem to be so godly.

God forsakes no people, but people forsake God when they 16.23 give away their power and claim not their birthright. Your birthright is simply the right to be who you are, and there is nothing in the world that has the power to take this right from you. The only way you lose it is by giving it away. And this you do.

God wants no sacrifice from you, yet when you give away 16.24 your power you make of yourself a sacrificial lamb, an offer- ing unto God that God does not want. You look back on stories of sacrifice from the Bible and think what a barbaric time that was, and yet you repeat the same history but in different form. If a talented physician were to give up his power to heal you would surely call it a waste, and yet you give up your power to be who you are and think it is just the way life is. You give away your power and then bow down to those whom you have given it to, for you are afraid of nothing more than your own power.

16.25   This fear but stems from what you have used your power for. You know your power created the world of illusion in which you live, and so you think another must be able to do it better. You no longer trust yourself with your own power, and so you have forgotten it and realize not how important it is for it to be reclaimed. As good as you may want to be, you would still go meekly through your life trying to comply with rules of God and man with thought of some greater good in mind. If everyone did what he or she wanted to do, you reason, society would collapse and anarchy would rule. You think you are only fair in deciding that if everyone cannot do what they would want, then you, too, must abdicate your wishes for the common good. You thus behave in "noble" ways that serve no purpose.

16.26   If you cannot claim at least a small amount of love for your own Self, then neither can you claim your power, for they go hand in hand. There is no "common good" as you perceive of it, and you are not here to assure the continuance of society. The worries that would occupy you can be let go if you but work instead for the return of heaven and the return of your own Self.

17 CONSCIOUS
NON-PLANNING

Being who you are is no luxury reserved for the idle rich, or the very young or old. Being who you are is necessary for the completion of the universe. — 17.1

Being who you are is no luxury reserved for the idle rich, or 17.1
the very young or old. Being who you are is necessary for the
completion of the universe. Without the real you in it, there
would be a void within the universe — and this would be
impossible. And yet there is a way in which you are missing.

This has to do with consciousness and what you are aware 17.2
of. Let's just say the space that you would fill as your own
self is held for you by another part of your consciousness
that has never left it. It is the reunion of these two selves that
will bring about the completion of the universe and the
return of heaven. *Where two are joined together* can be used
rightly here as well as in regard to relationship. Your choice
to separate from God is but a separation from your own Self,
and this is truly the separation that needs to be healed to
return you to God.

You shy away from thoughts of a consciousness beyond that 17.3
which you are aware of because of fear. And yet you know
you cannot claim that you are aware of all that exists within

the universe, or even that you fully know your own self. What is fearful about the unknown is simply that it is unknown. Coming to know what was previously unknown to you can remove the fear, if you will let it.

17.4   Consciousness of which you are unaware is not magic, superstition, or insanity. Yet you shield yourself from knowledge of it as if it would change the nature of the universe itself. It will change your perception of it. This is both what you desire and what you fear just as you both desire and fear knowing yourself.

17.5   There is an underlying assumption that you know all that is good for you to know, and that to know more is going to mean that things you would rather not know, and therefore must be *bad,* are what will be revealed. And yet all the evidence of your own thoughts will reveal to you your willingness to accept the *bad* about yourself and your world. And so this assumption that what is unknown must be bad cannot be valid, even by your own standards of evidence. Yet, in your estimation, the unknown cannot be fully good or worthy of your knowing because the reason that you use is loyal to the world you see. This is why even Heaven, which you would label good, is not wholly good in your estimation of it. Why is it not wholly good? Because you have defined it as lacking much of what you have judged to be good in the world you now perceive.

17.6   You have, however, willingly entered many unknown states. Some of you have gotten married, had children, taken mind-altering drugs, or attempted strenuous or even terrifying physical feats. But all of you without exception have willingly entered the unknown state of sleep and experienced the loss of consciousness that it brings. Each of you has had the experience of dreaming during the time of sleep.

Some may claim they know everything there is to know about sleep and dreaming, being married, using drugs, or having children; but even those of you who would listen to what the experts have to say believe this not.

Each day is an unknown you enter into, despite your every attempt to anticipate what it might hold. And yet while it would seem you would grow quite used to this phenomenon, you do not. You still make your plans and rail against everything that interferes with them, even knowing in advance that your greatest efforts at organization are often to no avail. *A Course in Miracles* asks you to "receive instead of plan," and yet few of you understand the meaning of this simple instruction or what it says to you of the unknown.

17.7

What it says is that the unknown is benevolent. What it says is that what you cannot anticipate can be anticipated for you. What it says is that you could be receiving constant help if you would but let it come. What it says is that you are not alone.

17.8

Receiving implies that something is being given. Receiving implies a willingness to accept what is given. This willingness is what you do not offer. Yet this is due to your lack of understanding about the nature of creation, and can be corrected.

17.9

Sin is simply the belief that correction cannot be made. This is the mistake that has happened in creation. This is how the impossible has become possible. If you were not so determined to believe correction cannot be made, correction would have occurred. This is the original error that is so in need of correction: your belief in sin — or in other words, your belief that what you have chosen is not reversible.

17.10

17.11   Is this not evident in the judgment you rely upon and in your treatment of criminals as well as of your own self and those you love? You believe mistakes must be paid for, not once but many times, and no matter how heavy the payment is, it only "pays for" what was done and cannot ever be undone. What does payment do but purchase something that is then yours to keep? What have you purchased with all your effort to make amends for your wrongdoing? You have but purchased guilt, and hold it to yourself — a constant companion and a judgment on your own self.

17.12   See you now why those who judge cannot enter heaven? Judgment proceeds from the belief in sin and the irreversibility of all errors. If you do not believe you can reverse or "turn back" to the state in which you existed before the original error, then you never shall.

17.13   And yet all you need do is turn back. Being an observer of your body has prepared you for this. Step back now to the place that has been held for you. You have not lost "your place in line" because you wandered. It has been held for you by the most loving of brothers, a brother united with your own Self.

17.14   This space you can turn back to holds no judgment and no fear, and so it is the repository of all that has proceeded from love. There it keeps all love's gifts safe for you. Love's gifts are gifts of creation or extension, gifts you have both given and received. Each act of love is added to the space in the universe that is yours and has become part of the whole along with you. All that has proceeded from fear is nothing, and has no existence apart from your own thoughts.

17.15   Your thoughts, however, have become quite harsh, and quite entrenched in the belief in their right to judge. Many of you have let go your belief in sin and still held on to your belief in judgment, thinking one is different from the other. They are not different, and while you do not see this your thoughts remain based on fear and fear thus remains your foundation. For judgment is but the belief that what God created can be changed, and has been.

Yet forgiveness, which replaces judgment, must come from   17.16
your heart. To forgive based on the logic of your mind rather than the compassion of your heart is to only give thought to forgiveness. This many of you will give, even to deciding to forgive despite your better judgment. See you not how little sense this makes, how insincere this even sounds?

Sincerity is synonymous with wholeheartedness — a con-   17.17
cept you do not understand for it is beyond concepts. But now we begin to integrate your learning as we move to wholeness. The first move toward wholeness is but to under-stand this: heart and mind are not separate. A united mind and heart is a whole heart, or wholeheartedness. You may ask then why this Course has treated them as separate parts of you. This is simply because this is the way you see them, and because it has allowed me to address the different func-tions you have given them.

Yet, what is the same cannot have different functions. And   17.18
now your mind and heart must work together in the united function we have established — returning to you your iden-tity within God's creation.

CHAPTER **18** | the MIND ENGAGED

Wholeheartedness is but a full expression of your power. A full expression of your power is creation. What has been created cannot be uncreated. What has been created can, however, be transformed. Transformation occurs in time. Thus transformation and miracles need to work hand in hand. — 18.18

Many of you believe God's creation included the fall from 18.1
paradise as described in the biblical story of Adam and Eve
and in the creation stories of many cultures and religions.
When you accept this, even in nonliteral terms, as the story
of the separation, you accept separation itself. This story is,
rather than a story of an actual event, a story that describes
the problem. It is but the story of perception's birth. And
your perception of the fall makes of the fall a curse. This
interpretation would be inconsistent, however, with a benevolent God and a benevolent universe. This interpretation
accepts that separation can occur. It cannot. Belief in the fall
is belief in the impossible.

Imagine that you are part of a chain of bodies holding hands 18.2
and encircling the globe. I am among those whose hand you
hold. All are linked, even if each one is not holding the hand
of every other one. If one link in the chain were to be
removed, the chain would no longer form a circle but would
"fall," each end suspended in space. The chain would now be
a line seeming to go from here to there, instead of enclosing

and encompassing everything. The separation assumes that you can break the chain. This would be as impossible as it would be for me to let go of your hand.

18.3   Now imagine further that this chain is keeping the Earth in its orbit. It is obvious that the Earth falling out of orbit would cause dire consequences of a universal nature. It is simply less obvious that you are part of what has established and keeps a universal order, part of a whole that would be a completely different whole without your presence, just as the universe would be a completely different universe without the presence of the Earth.

18.4   Yet this is, in effect, what you think you have done. You think that you have changed the nature of the universe and made it possible for life to exist separately and alone with no relationship, no connection, no unity with the whole. This you have not done. You have not "fallen" from unity. You have not "fallen" from God.

18.5   This chain I have described helps you to imagine the place I hold for you, as you held mine when I entered the world in physical form. Even if it is just an illustration, it illustrates that none of us leave wholeness or each other.

18.6   While you have been taught that you are not your body, it is impossible for you to deny the body here. Yet you can change the function you have ascribed to it, and so its way of functioning. If you do not see it as the result of a fall, as a curse, as a punishment from God, or as your home, a dwelling place that keeps you separate, then you can begin to see it as what it is, a learning device given you by a loving creator. Before the idea of separation, there was no need for learning. But a loving creator creates not that which can have a need go unfulfilled. As soon as the need for learning arose, the perfect

means to fulfill that need was established. You have simply
failed to see it as such.

This is the error birthed by perception, before which there   18.7
was no possibility of misinterpretation, because there was no
external world to be perceived. A learning device, when not
perceived as such, holds not much hope of fulfilling the function it was created to fulfill. But when perception changes
and a thing is seen as what it is, then it cannot fail to accomplish what it was created to accomplish.

An external world is but a projection that cannot take you   18.8
away from the internal world where you exist in wholeness, a
link in the chain of creation. Imagine again this chain and
yourself among those who comprise it, and imagine the life
that you experience now taking place much like that you
would see projected on a movie screen. You have not left your
place as you view this movie and experience its sights and
sounds, joys and sorrows. And yet you are also part of the
projection, and this is where your awareness now abides,
seemingly trapped upon the screen, viewing everything from
the two eyes of the one projected there. Again, this is but
what this Course's exercises have attempted to help you see:
a world you can observe and learn in and from, for as long as
you would choose to learn what the idea of separation would
teach you. Making a new choice, a choice to learn from
unity, is what this Course prepares you for.

Learning from unity requires an integrated mind and heart,   18.9
or wholeheartedness. A half-hearted approach to this learning will not work, nor will the attention of a split mind. It
cannot be emphasized strongly enough that you learn what
you choose to learn. For proof of this all you need do is look
at the world that was created from your wish to learn what
the idea of separation would teach you. When you resided in

unity, you could not imagine what this world would be like any more than you can now imagine what a united world will be like. You did not understand, from unity's standpoint, what it was that you were asking for, or the extent of involvement this learning would require. In order to learn what the idea of separation would teach you, you needed to believe that you existed in a separated state. Thus, "forgetting" that you actually reside in unity was a requirement of this condition you wished to experience. This condition was thus made available.

18.10   While this explanation makes perfect sense, you find it quite unbelievable on the basis of your perception of yourself and the limited range of power you believe your decision making to have. The only way to make the unbelievable believable is to alter what you experience. The state in which you now exist was not only unbelievable but also inconceivable to you in your natural state. Experience was required in order to alter your belief system and is required now as well.

18.11   The experience of unity will alter your belief system and that of others, for what you learn in unity is shared. Because you are currently learning from separation, however, each must experience unity individually before their belief system can be changed even when what is learned is shared at another level.

18.12   Perception of levels is a function of time, and thus it seems that great amounts of time are needed before change of a lasting nature can occur. This is why miracles save time, for they integrate all levels, temporarily collapsing time. Time is actually a measurement of learning, or the "time" it takes for learning to pass from one level to another through experience, for here learning is experienced in time.

In order for your experience base to change from that of   18.13
learning in separation to that of learning in unity, learning
from what unity can teach you must be birthed as an idea. To
hear or learn of another's idea is not to give birth to it. You
thus must each experience the birth of the idea of learning
from unity in order for it to come from within and leave not
its Source. An idea of mine can only become an idea of yours
through your relationship with it. You need only to experience this idea in your own way, from the desire to know from
which all ideas are born, in order to give it life.

Once an idea is born, it exists in relationship to its creator.   18.14
All that remains now is a choice of participation. In unity, all
that you desired was participated in fully by a mind and heart
combined in wholeheartedness. You knew your Self to be the
creator, and loved all that you created. You did not desire and
fear something at the same time, and your desires did not
change from moment to moment. What you desired you
experienced fully with your whole being, making it one with
you. That you keep yourself from desiring anything fully here
is what makes this existence so chaotic and erratic. A mind
and heart in conflict is what keeps you from desiring anything fully, and thus from creating.

Thus, the integration of mind and heart must be our goal in   18.15
order for you to create the state in which unity can be experienced. Obviously, this is up to you. As you chose to create
a state of separation, you must choose to create a state of
unity.

It can come as no surprise to you that your mind has ruled   18.16
your heart. What this course has thus far attempted to do is
to briefly change your orientation from mind to heart. This
is a first step in what will seem now like an attempt to balance two separate things, but is really an attempt to unite

what you have only perceived as separate. If the heart is the center of your Self, where then is the mind? The center is but the source in which all exist as one mind. To say this to you before we loosened some of your perceptions about the supremacy of the mind, however, would have been folly. The one mind is not as you have perceived *your* mind. The one mind is but a mind in which love rules, and mind and heart are one. We will proceed by calling this wholehearted-ness rather than mind or heart.

18.17   A wandering mind is seen as quite the norm, and thoughts that dart about in a chaotic fashion are as acceptable and seemingly as inevitable to you as breathing. A split mind is seen as not much less normal although it is recognized that a split mind makes decision making difficult. You were already told that the only exercise for your mind that would be included in this Course of Love is that you dedicate all thought to union. This now must be seen in two dimensions rather than one. In addition to dedicating thought to unity with the whole, you must dedicate yourself to unifying thought itself.

18.18   You do not realize what a wholehearted choice in regards to experiencing separation did. Wholeheartedness is but a full expression of your power. A full expression of your power is creation. What has been created cannot be uncreated. What has been created can, however, be transformed. Transformation occurs in time. Thus transformation and miracles need to work hand in hand.

18.19   The transformation from a state of separation to a state of unity is a miracle indeed, for this transformation requires recognition of a state that you cannot recognize in separa-tion. While this is a paradox, it is not impossible for the simple reason that you never left the state of unity that you do not recognize. Your lack of recognition can thus be overcome by remembering the truth of what you are.

Unifying thought is more than a matter of focus or single-mindedness, although these are both steps in the right direction. Unifying thought is also a matter of integrating the thought or language of your heart with that which you more naturally perceive as thought, the words and images that "go through" your mind. 18.20

We talked briefly here of emotions, doing so only to differentiate your feelings of love from your feelings of lack of love or fear. What we have as yet talked even less of, however, is what emotion covers up, and the stillness that lies beneath. I have referred to the true language of the heart as communion, or union of the highest level, and of remembrance of who you are being the means by which communion can return to you. So what we speak of now is integrating remembrance and thought. 18.21

While we spoke of what you think of as emotion being reactions of the body to stimulus, we did not speak of this stimulus itself. Before we do so, we must clarify further the function of the body as a learning device. Your body seems to experience both pleasure and pain, yet as a learning device, it is neutral. It does not experience, but only conveys that which can be experienced to you. You then relay a reaction back to it. This circular relationship between you and the body is the perfect relationship for the purpose of learning, since both the experience and the reaction to the experience can then be learned from, and because the learner can choose both. It is not, however, the perfect relationship when you have misperceived the body as your home rather than as a learning device. Because you have misperceived the body as your home, there is, in a sense, no "you" to which the body 18.22

can send its signals. And so the body seems to be in charge and to be both the experiencer and the interpreter of experience. In addition, this misperception has allowed the body's function to go unrecognized. You thus have not recognized the truth of what causes pain nor that you can reject the experience of it. The same is true of pleasure.

18.23   Determination of pleasure and pain is made with the judgment of the separated self who not only believes it is the body, but that it is at the body's mercy. Yet the body has no mercy to offer the separated self. It is only a learning device. But you have not recognized this and have failed to learn that all you experience as painful is the result of feelings of lack of love, and that all you have experienced as pleasurable are feelings of love. This would seem to contradict what was said earlier about the pain experienced from love and your willingness to cling to it despite the pain you are experiencing. Yet the pain comes not from your feelings of love, but feelings of love lost.

18.24   Having no one to receive and reject feelings of pain and replace them with feelings of love causes all your distress. Think not that you react to pain of any kind with the love from your real Self that would dispel it. The Self you have taken out of the learning loop is the Self of love.

Each one of your brothers and sisters is as holy as I and as beloved of God. Can you not witness to their belovedness as those long ago witnessed to mine? You have not been able to do this thus far because you have desired specialness for yourself and a few others rather than belovedness for all. But now, perhaps, you are ready. — 19.9

There was no evil intent in the creation of the body as a 19.1 learning device, and as a learning device it was perfectly created. The problem lies in what you have, in your forgetfulness, made of the body. Only from thinking of the body as yourself did ideas of glorifying the body arise. To glorify a learning device makes no sense. And yet in creating the perfect device from which you could experience separation, all such problems were anticipated and corrective devices created alongside them. You could not fully experience separation without a sense of self as separate, and you could not fully experience anything without your free will. A separate self with a free will operating in an external world, as well as a spirit self desiring the experience of separation, would naturally lead to a situation where the whole range of experiences available to a separate being would exist.

The complex set of criteria needed to create a world of sepa- 19.2 ration was, in the instant of creation, anticipated and provided in a form consistent with creation's laws. While this world was created with love, as all of creation was, it was also created to provide the desired experience. Thus was fear born, for a separate self is a fearful self by its nature. How could it not be?

19.3 You who have grown weary of this experience rejoice, for you can choose a new experience. Your free will has not been taken from you, nor has the power of creation abandoned you. Within creation's own laws does the solution rest.

19.4 The solution lies in transformation, and that is why you are still needed here. Beneath the world of illusion that you have made to glorify the separated self lies the world that was created for your learning, and that so exists in truth. It is not the only world by any means, but it is still heaven because heaven must be where you are. A wholehearted choice to abandon all ideas of glorifying the separated self and to let the world be what it is will begin the transformation. This requires the first unification, the unification of mind and heart, after which unification with God is naturally returned to your awareness, for this unification returns you to the Christ in you and the one mind united with God that you have never left. Creation's power then returns to you to help all the separated ones remember union.

19.5 Although this all may sound like science fiction to you, realize that you accept much in all areas of your life, from that of religion to science itself, that sounds like fiction. You are not, however, expected to believe all I have told you on faith alone. Experience is needed to change your beliefs and place your faith securely in them. The first step in leading you to experience of another kind is your willingness to accept that you are here to learn, and that your body can provide the means.

19.6 Your saving grace is that even a separated self yearns for union and knowledge of its creator. Thus along with this yearning was a means provided for its fulfillment, and with this fulfillment lies the end of the separation.

I was part of this means, but only part. Fulfillment can be provided by each and every one of your brothers and sisters, for in each is the Christ available to be seen and experienced as it was from me. It is in your holy relationships that union can be found and experienced, and thus from these that you fuel your desire for union with all and for knowledge of your creator. This yearning must but be a pure yearning — untainted by fear and judgment and approached with wholeheartedness — for it to be fulfilled. It is not the means that are lacking but the wholehearted desire. 19.7

Let me speak briefly of the role I played so that you can better understand the role that waits for you. I came in the fulfillment of scripture. All this really means is that a certain community had been led to expect my arrival. They awaited me with expectation and so found in me what they hoped to find. What my brothers and sisters saw in me allowed me to be who I was, even while in human form. I tell you truly if you were to see any of your brothers and sisters today as those who awaited my birth saw me, they too would remember who they are. This is the role I ask you to accept so that you can provide for others what was provided for me. 19.8

Each one of your brothers and sisters is as holy as I and as beloved to God. Can you not witness to their belovedness as those long ago witnessed to mine? You have not been able to do this thus far because you have desired specialness for yourself and a few others rather than belovedness for all. But now, perhaps, you are ready. 19.9

The separated self cannot relearn unity except through union. Here, union is achieved in relationship. To see your 19.10

brothers and sisters as those of long ago saw me is the way to achieve relationship of the highest order and relearn communion, the language of the heart. This is why you have been asked to experience the spirit of your brothers and sisters rather than simply relating to their bodies as you always have. I was not seen as a body by those who believed in me, although I had a body to help me learn just as you do.

19.11　My testimony witnessed to your arrival just as the scriptures witnessed to mine. Even while some of my words were distorted or misinterpreted, you can still revisit them and see that this is so. I did not proclaim myself to be above or different from the rest, but called each of you brother and sister and reminded you of our Father's love and of our union with Him.

19.12　Your belief in your brothers and sisters will not be total, however, without the reunion of mind and heart that produces the state of wholeheartedness. This state was not achieved at all times by all those who believed in me — and perfection is not asked of you. As can be clearly seen from the records left to you, the apostles did not, in fact, achieve this state during my lifetime, for they looked at me as different and looked to me for power. Only after my resurrection did the Holy Spirit come upon them and reveal their own power to them by uniting mind and heart with belief. They were then reunited with me as they were united with the Christ. You thus must learn to see yourself as you see your brothers and sisters, and place your belief not in differences but in sameness.

19.13　In order to do this there is still one more layer to the unification of thought, and this brings up another reason for our reliance on the heart. Thought, as you know it, is an aspect of duality. It cannot be otherwise in your separated state. You must think in terms of "I" and "them," "death and life," "good and evil." This *is* thought. Thought occurs in words, and words separate. It is only in combining mind and heart with a focus on letting the heart lead that love can be combined with thought in such a way as to actually transcend thought as you know it. This transcendence is a function of wholeheartedness.

This is, in essence, why the greatest thinkers have not been able to decipher the riddle, the mystery, of the divine, and why they conclude that God is unknowable. Yet God is knowable from within the mystery of nonduality itself. It would be impossible for you to be a being that can yearn for knowledge of your Creator without this knowledge being available. In creation, all needs are fulfilled the instant they become needs, which is why there are no needs. If everything you need has been provided, having needs makes no sense. 19.14

Philosophy applies thought to mystery and that is why philosophy becomes such a muddle of words. It is difficult for you to accept that what you most need to know cannot be achieved through the same methods you have used in order to know about other things. And, increasingly, you are willing to exchange experience for secondhand knowledge and to believe you can come to know through the experiences of others. Yet, in the case of coming to know what lies before you now, coming to know your own self, it is obvious that another's experience will not bring this knowledge to you, not even my experience. If this were so, all of those who read of my life and words would have learned what I learned from my experience. While many have learned much of others, this type of learning is but a starting point, a gateway to experience. 19.15

19.16   To think without thought or know without words are ideas quite foreign to you, and truly, while you remain here, even experiences beyond thoughts and words you will apply word and thought to. Yet love has often brought you close to a "thought-less" and "word-less" state of being, and it can do so again. As you join with your own Self in unity, all that in love you have created and received returns to its home in you, and leaves you in a state of love in which the wordless and formless is very near.

19.17   Your only concept of oneness is of a single form, a single entity. There is either one chair or two. One table or four. Your emphasis has been on quantity, and one is seen as less than any other number. Yet, on the other hand, when only one of anything exists it is highly prized. God is thus "God" due, at least in part, to what you view as His singularity. You view those who worship many gods as primitive, although those who believe in a god synonymous with creation are closer to a true picture of God than those who view God as a solitary figure. Still, oneness and unity go together, the unity of creation being part of the oneness of God, and the oneness of God part of the unity of creation. A mind trained by separation can have no concept of this, as all concepts are born from the mind's separate thoughts. Yet this same mind could still conceive of a creator. A mind that can conceive of a creator combined with a heart than yearns for knowledge of, and union with, that creator, can bypass the need for the separate thoughts of the separated one's thought system. But you must be trained to do this. Thus your training begins. And begins with prayer.

19.18   As was said in the beginning, praying is asking. You but asked for your separated state and it was made so. Now you need to but ask for unity to return for it to be so. The condition or state of being from which you ask is what is in need of adjustment and thus of training before you can be aware of the answer you will receive. It is clear you can ask for what you know not. This is not the problem. The problem is in who is doing the asking. The separated self, while capable of asking, is hardly capable of believing in or accepting the response. It is this nonbelief in a response that makes it capable of asking. Now that you are beginning to shed the concept of the separate self and to believe in the possibility of response, you will find yourself more afraid to ask. All your asking or prayer awaits is but your belief in the love without fear that has always responded.

Out of the deepest, darkest chaos of your mind comes the possibility of light. It is a bit like traveling backwards, or the review of life that some experience after death. In order to remember unity you must, in a sense, travel back to it, undoing as you go all you have learned since last you knew it, so all that remains is love. This undoing, or atonement, has begun — and once begun is unstoppable and thus already inevitably accomplished.

19.19

My brothers and sisters in Christ, do not become impatient now. We are on the home stretch and all you long for is nearer than ever before. To talk of going "back" will undoubtedly make you feel impatient, but this is not a going back that will in any way resemble the "going back" that you have tried to do before. While it is, in a sense, a request to review your life, it is the last such review that will be required before letting the past go completely. All your previous attempts to go back have been like attempts to pay a debt that will never go away. This going back will leave you debt free and thus free in truth.

19.20

This going back is the journey without distance. You need not go in search of it, and in truth, cannot, for the past does

19.21

not abide in you. What you need rather do is strive for a place of stillness from which what needs review can arise as if it were a reflection arising from a deep pool. Here what is in need of healing will but briefly come to the surface and leave the hidden depths where light could not reach it and healing could not come. What comes forth for healing needs but a nod of love from your heart, a passing glance of compassion, the merest moment of reflection, before it will dissipate and show a new reflection.

19.22   This going back is, in reality, more in the way of reflection than review, although if you were to think of this as a reviewing of your self, you would be quite accurate. It is like unto the final judgment as it has been described, a sorting of the real from the unreal, of truth from illusion. Despite the similarity between what this will call forth and the description of the final judgment, judgment is not the means or end of this reckoning.

19.23   The loftiest aim of which you are currently capable is that of changing your perception. Although our ultimate goal is to move beyond perception to knowledge, a first step in doing this is changing your means of perception to that of right-mindedness. Your willingness to accept me as your teacher will help you to accept my sight as your own and thus to be right-minded. The way you have perceived of yourself and your world until now has not been right-minded, and you are beginning to realize this. Thus it is now appropriate for the realization to come to you that your mind, and your perception, can be changed. This is necessary before you can look back in a new way and not simply cover the same ground you have covered a million times, seeing causes for recriminations, blame, and guilt. Looking back in judgment is not what is required here. Only the opposite will advance our aim of uniting mind and heart.

The Holy Spirit exists in your right mind, and is the bridge   19.24
to exchanging perception for knowledge. Knowledge is
light, and the only light in which you can truly see. You will
not truly desire to unite your mind and heart in wholeheartedness until you see clearly. One purpose of the distinctions you have made between mind and heart are their
ability to keep one part of yourself blameless. Whatever happens, your divided notion of yourself allows you to both
protect and conceal. Fault always lies elsewhere. The guilt-
less part of you is always free to redeem the guilt-filled self.
This idea of self-redemption has long been a culprit that has
kept union, even with your own self, undesirable to you.
The concept that in oneness there is no need for blame or
guilt or even for redemption is inconceivable to the separate
mind. But not to the heart.

Love is the Source of your being. You flow from love, an outpouring without end. You are thus eternal. You are pure and innocent because you flow from love. What flows from love is changeless and boundless. You are without limit.

— 20.27

Your longing now has reached a fever pitch, a burning in your heart quite different from that which you have felt before. Your heart may even feel as if it is stretching outward, straining heavenward, near to bursting with its desire for union, a desire you do not understand but can surely feel. 20.1

This is a call to move now into my embrace and let yourself be comforted. Let the tears fall and the weight of your shoulders rest upon mine. Let me cradle your head against my breast as I stroke your hair and assure you that it will be all right. Realize that this is the whole world, the universe, the all of all in whose embrace you literally exist. Feel the gentleness and the love. Drink in the safety and the rest. Close your eyes and begin to see with an imagination that is beyond thought and words. 20.2

You are no longer the object viewing the subjects of the kingdom. You are the heart of the kingdom. The kingdom's beauty revealed. The beloved child suckled at the breast of the queen mother earth, one child of one mother, nameless 20.3

and beyond naming. No "I" resides here. You have given up the vision of your eyes and the "I" of your ego. You are loosed of bounds, no longer a thing of beauty, but beauty itself.

20.4   "Thingness" is over, and your identity no longer stands in form but flows from life itself. Your beauty is the gathering of the atoms, the order in chaos, the silence in solitude, the grace of the cosmos. Our heart is the light of the world.

20.5   We are one heart.

20.6   We are one mind. One creative force gathering the atoms, establishing the order, blessing the silence, gracing the cosmos, manifesting the light of the heart. Here we live as one body, experiencing communion, the soul's delight, rather than otherness. It is a seamless world, a tapestry where each thread is vibrant and strong. A canticle where each tone is pure and indivisible.

20.7   We have returned to the embrace. And now your arms cradle me as well, for an embrace, although it may begin with one reaching out to another, concludes with mutuality, shared touch, a melding of one into another. The embrace makes one of two.

20.8   And now we begin to see with the eyes of our heart. We are no longer looking "out" but looking "in." All landscapes and horizons form within the embrace. All beauty resides there. All light is fused and infused within the embrace. Within the embrace our sight clears and what we see is known rather than understood.

20.9   Here, rest comes to weariness and gently lays it aside. Time has ended and there is nothing you must do. Being replaces identity and you say, *I am. I am*, and there is nothing outside of me. Nothing outside of the embrace.

From here your life becomes imaginal, a dream that requires   20.10
you not to leave your home, your place of safety and of rest.
You are cradled gently while your spirit soars, dreaming
happy dreams at last. With love surrounding you in arms that
hold you close, you feel the heartbeat of the world just
beneath your resting head. It thunders in your ears and
moves through you until there is no distinction. We are the
heartbeat of the world.

This is creation. This is God. This is our home.   20.11

We exist in the embrace of love like the layers of light that   20.12
form a rainbow, indivisible and curved inward upon each
other. Love grows from within as a child grows within its
mother's womb. Inward, inward, into the embrace, the
source of all beginnings, the kernel and the wholeness of all
life. The whole exists untroubled by what it will be. It is.

The time of parables has ended. A new time of no time   20.13
awaits. Nothing is like unto anything else. Likeness, like
thingness, has been overcome with oneness. Oneness pre-
vails. The reign of Christ is at hand.

I am alive and you do believe this or you would not be here.   20.14
Yet you think not of me living and imagine it not. Christ
reigns in the kingdom in which I live just as Christ reigned
within me on earth. In the cave on this earth where my dead
body was laid, the Christ in me returned me to the embrace.
The singular heartbeat of the man Jesus no longer sounded.
My heartbeat was the heartbeat of the world.

Imagine a body in a cave, a cave in the earth, the earth in the   20.15
planet, the planet in the universe. Each cradles the other.
None are passive. None are dead. All share the heartbeat
of the world and are at rest within each other, within
each other's embrace and the embrace of God's love, God's

creation, God's heartbeat. God's heartbeat is the Source of the world, the Soul of the world, the Sound of the world in harmony, existence with no beginning and no end. One embrace. All in all. None lesser and none greater for all is all. One is one.

20.16   There is no longer cause for alienation, nor for the feeling of abandonment so many of you have felt. You are now within the embrace where all such hurts are healed.

20.17   The world does not exist apart from you, and so you must realize your compassionate connection. The world is not a collection of cement buildings and paved streets nor of cold, heartless people who would as soon do you harm as good. It is but the place of your interaction with all that lives within you, sharing the one heartbeat. The heartbeat of the world does not exist apart from God. The heartbeat of the world is thus alive and part of you. This heart connection is what we seek to return you to. This realization that the world is not a "thing," as you are not a "thing." Your identity is shared and one in Christ. A shared identity is a quality of oneness. A shared identity is one identity. When you identify with Christ you identify with the one identity. When you realize the oneness of your identity you will be one with Christ. Christ is synonymous with oneness.

20.18   Who could be left out of the embrace? And who from within the embrace could be separate and alone?

20.19   Have you never felt as if you would wrap your arms around the world and bring it comfort if you could? This you can do. Not with physical arms, but with the arms of love. Have you never cried for the state of the world as you would for one small child in need of love? Has the world then not lost its thingness? And has it not as well lost its personalness? Are your tears not shed for what lives and breathes and exists along with you? And is the you who sheds such tears a personal being? A thing? A mass of flesh and bone? Or are you, like the world you cry for, devoid of thingness and a personal self? And when you have leapt for joy at the world's beauty, has it not leapt with you, returning grace for grace?

Is it possible to have a concept of wholeness, of "all," and for it not to exist? And how could it exist apart from you? Oneness with Christ, dear brother and sister, is nothing more than this concept realized. And also nothing less.   20.20

This lesson is only as complicated as the most complex among you needs it to be. But for some it can be simple, as simple as realizing the oneness of the embrace. Within the embrace you can let all thought go. Within the embrace, you can quit thinking even of holy things, holy men and women, and even divine beings, even the one God. Is not the embrace itself holy? Is not the sunrise and sunset? Is not the least of the birds of the air as holy as the mighty eagle? The blade of grass, the fleck of sand, the wind and air, the ocean and her surf, all live by the universal heartbeat and exist within the embrace. Is not all you can imagine holy when you imagine with love? Is not all you cannot imagine holier still?   20.21

Sanctity is all that exists within the embrace. How could you be less than sacred? You exist in holiness.   20.22

The first step in remembering this holiness is forgetting. Let yourself forget that you do not feel holy and that the world does not appear to be sacred. Let your heart remember that you are holy and that the world is sacred. A thousand things   20.23

can pull you from your remembrance. Forgetting "things" can free you to remember.

20.24　Forget yourself and memory will return to you. Beyond your personal self and the identity you have given your personal self is your being. This is the face of Christ where all being resides. This is your true identity.

20.25　Thankfulness is the nature of your being. It could not be otherwise when awe and magnificence encompass you in the embrace. Your heart sings in gratitude for the all that you are. You are the beauty of the world and peace abides within you.

20.26　Peace is the foundation of your being. Not a peace that implies an absence but a peace that implies a fullness. Wholeness is peaceful. Only separation creates conflict.

20.27　Love is the Source of your being. You flow from love, an outpouring without end. You are thus eternal. You are pure and innocent because you flow from love. What flows from love is changeless and boundless. You are without limit.

20.28　Power is the expression of who you are. Because you are changeless and boundless, you are all-powerful. Only lack of expression leads to powerlessness. No true expression is possible until you know who you are. To know who you are and not to express who you are with your full power is the result of fear. To know the safety and love of the embrace is to know no cause for fear, and thus to come into your true power. True power is the power of miracles.

20.29　Miracles are expressions of love. You might think of them as acts of cooperation. Holiness cannot be contained, and it is not within your power to limit it. To feel the holiness of the embrace is to release its power. While expression and action are not the same, understanding their relationship to each other is essential.

Expressions of love are as innumerable as the stars in the universe, as bountiful as beauty, as many faceted as the gems of the earth. I say again that sameness is not a sentence to mediocrity or uniformity. You are a unique expression of the selfsame love that exists in all creation. Thus your expression of love is as unique as your Self. It is in the cooperation between unique expressions of love that creation continues and miracles become natural occurrences.   20.30

This cooperation is natural when fear has been rejected. You have long embraced fear and rejected love. Now the reverse is true. This reversal of truth has changed the nature of your universe and the laws by which it operates. The laws of fear were laws of struggle, limits, danger, and competitiveness. The laws of love are laws of peace, abundance, safety, and cooperation. Your actions and the results of your actions in a universe of love will naturally be different from your actions and the results of your actions in a universe of fear. You set the laws of the universe when you chose fear. The laws of the universe of love are God given.   20.31

Acceptance of your true power is acceptance of your God-given authority via your free will. When I beseeched my Father, saying, *"They know not what they do,"* I was expressing the nature of my brothers and sisters as caused by fear. To accept your power and your God-given authority is to know what you do. Let the fear be taken from this area of your thought so that you can see the application of cooperative action. As long as you fear your own ability to know what you do, you cannot be fully cooperative.   20.32

20.33　　The rest of the universe, existing in a state of compassionate free will devoid of fear, knows what it does. There are no opposing forces that are not in agreement about their opposing force. No atoms do battle. No molecules compete for dominance. The universe is a dance of cooperation. You are but asked to rejoin the dance.

20.34　　The embrace has returned you to attunement with the heartbeat, the music of the dance. You have not known what you do or what to do only because of fear, only because you have been out of accord with the one heartbeat. The world, the universe, is your partner — and only now do you hear the music that brings grace to all your movements, all your actions, all your expressions of love. While this may seem to be metaphorical language it is not. Listen and you will hear. Hear, and you cannot help but rejoice in the dance.

20.35　　You have not before now been able to even imagine knowing what you do. You hope to have moments of clarity concerning what you are doing in a given moment, what you have done, what you hope to do in the future. But even these moments of clarity are fractional. They seldom have any relation to the whole. Knowing what you do comes from existing within the embrace. You know you do the will of God because you are at one with that will.

20.36　　Bitterness and uncertainty are replaced by hope. Hope is the condition of the initiate, new to the realization of having a home within the embrace. It is the response that says to all you have just read, "Ah, if only it were true. If only it *could* be true." Notice the complete change in this "if only" from those we have spoken of earlier — the "if onlys" of fear. If you put half as much faith in these "if onlys" as you have in the "if onlys" of fear, all the certainty I have spoken of will be yours.

Knowing what you do is a present moment knowing. It is not   20.37
about plans. It is about moment-by-moment knowing exactly
who you are and acting out of that loving identity, and it is
about knowing that as you do so you are in accord and enjoy-
ing the full cooperation of the entire universe.

Hope is a manner of acting as if the best possible outcome   20.38
you can imagine could truly occur. Hope is a willingness to
accept love and the grace and cooperation that flow from
love. Hope is a willingness to ask for help, believing it will
come. Hope is the reason and the outcome for which we
pray. Hope acknowledges the kindliness of the universe and
has no use for things. The inanimate as well as the animate is
called upon, depended upon for service. All use is replaced
with service, and appreciation replaces the callousness with
which use once occurred.

All service is cooperative and depends on a belief in mutual-   20.39
ity. All fear that what is good for one may not be good for the
whole is replaced by an understanding that each one is worthy of his or her desires. "Eachness" replaces "thingness" but
not oneness. All fear that what one gets means that less is
available for another is replaced with an understanding of
abundance. Receiving replaces all notions of taking or getting. All that is received is for the mutual benefit of all and
takes nothing away from anyone. There is no limit to love
and so there are no limits to anything that flows from love.
What one benefits from everyone benefits from.

Receiving is an act of mutuality. It stems from a basic law   20.40
of the universe expressed in the saying that the sun shines and
the rain falls on the good and evil alike. All gifts of God are
given equally and distributed equally. It is your belief that
this is not so that causes judgment. All who believe they have
"more" fall prey to righteousness. All who believe they

have "less" fall victim to envy. Both "fall" from grace and limit their ability to receive. No gifts are received when all gifts are judged. While the gift is still given, the judgment changes the nature of the gift by limiting its ability to be of service. A gift one feels one cannot "use" is discarded. Thus have many of your treasures lain fallow.

20.41   What you each have been given is that which will serve your purpose. You could have no more perfect gifts, for your gifts are expressions of your Father's perfect love for you. Look deep inside and feel your heart's gladness. Your construction was no mistake. You are not flawed. You are not wanting. You would not be other than you are except when you give in to making judgments. Look deeply and you will see that what you would call your imperfections are as chosen and as dear to you as all the rest.

20.42   You would not be other than who you are. You may know that this is true or you may dwell in fantasies, desiring what another has or some success, fame, or riches that seem impossible for you to attain. And yet, whether you know it is true or not, it is true: You would not be other than who you are. Herein lie your peace and your perfection. If you would not be other than you are, then you must be perfect. This is a conclusion both logical to the mind and believable to the heart, and its acceptance is a step toward wholeheartedness.

20.43   To believe in your perfection and the equality of your gifts is peaceful, because it releases you from trying to acquire that which you previously believed you were lacking. It releases you from judgment because you know that your brothers and sisters are also beings of perfection. When you begin to see them as such, what you will receive from them is far grander than anything you would before have wished to take from them.

Your thinking will begin to change to reflect your recognition   20.44
of reception. Reception and welcome are highly linked. You
will find you are welcome to all the gifts you recognize
in your brothers and sisters just as you freely will offer yours
to serve them. To serve rather than to use is an enormous
change in thinking, feeling, and acting. It will immediately
make the world a kinder, gentler place. And it is only a beginning.

To serve is different from your ideas of service, however. Your   20.45
ideas of service are bound to your ideas of charity. Your idea
of charity is based on some having more and some having
less. Thus, you must remain cognizant of this distinction
between serving and service. It will be helpful if you keep in
mind that the idea of *to serve* is being used to replace the idea
of *to use* and is its opposite. It replaces the thought of taking
with the thought of receiving. It implies that you are welcome to all the gifts of the universe and that they can be
given, through you, to others as well. It implies willingness
rather than resistance. To change your thinking and your
feelings from expecting resistance to expecting willingness is
another key change that will lead toward wholeheartedness.
When you change your actions from those of resistance and
use to those of being willing to serve and be served, it will
assist not only you and your peacefulness, but will bring
peacefulness to the world as well.

Before you begin to resist the notion that you could have   20.46
anything to do with world peace, realize that you naturally
have reacted with resistance. You must replace your willingness to believe in your inadequacy and smallness with your
willingness to believe in your ability and mightiness.
Remember not your ego concerns and remember instead the
warmth of the embrace. Remember not your personal identity but remember instead your shared identity.

20.47   Your personal concerns are concerns you have been taught to believe you have. They are small concerns and they are among the reasons for your belief in your inability to effect change within your own life and certainly within the greater life of the universe. You must understand that when you think of your personal life, personal concerns, personal relationships, you are separating yourself from the whole. These concerns are a matter of perception, and are things your mind has been trained to see as being within its scope. It is as if you have cordoned off a little section of life and said these are the things that relate to my existence and to me and they are all I need concern myself with. Even when you think of expanding your view, you deem that expansion unrealistic. You cannot do everything. You cannot effect world peace. You can barely keep your personal concerns in order. Your effort to do so is all that stands between you and chaos.

20.48   Your heart has a different scope, a different view. It is the view from within the embrace, the view from love's angle. It is the view of the dying who realize nothing matters but love. This realization is not one of sentiment, regrets, or wishful thinking. It is the view from the embrace, the return to one heartbeat, the return to what is known. This knowing you might call wisdom and think of as an attainable ideal of thought. Yet it is not about thought at all, but is beyond thought. It is not wisdom but the truth. The truth is that which exists. The false is illusion. Love is all that matters because love is all that is.

The embrace can now be likened to the starting point of a shared language, a language shared by mind and heart and by all people. It is a language of images and concepts that touch the one heart and serve the one mind. — 21.6

Love is. 21.1

Love is eternal, and you do not as yet grasp its meaning or 21.2 the meaning of eternity. This is because as a particular being you are time bound. You can realize the eternal even in your temporary form if you can let go of your particularity. Particularity has to do with mass, substance, form. Your being is far beyond your imagined reliance on the particular. The particular is about parts and parts are all you see. I remind you of what was said earlier concerning relationships existing apart from particulars. I repeat that relationship exists *between* one thing and another and that it is in the intersection of parts that the holiness of what is in between is found. This will be discussed in more detail later, but for now, I return you, through the embrace, to the holy relationship but in a broadened form.

The holy relationship in its broadened form is eternity, the 21.3 eternity of the embrace. If the embrace is the source of all, the one heartbeat, then it is eternity itself. It is the face of love, its texture, taste, and feel. It is love conceptualized. It is an abstract rather than a particular concept, even while having a seeming structure that your heart can feel. Concepts that cannot be felt with your heart are of no use to you now, for they are meant for their usefulness rather than for their service. Concepts that touch your heart serve you through this touch. They also begin to help break you away from the need for comparisons, for there is no need to compare what your heart can feel. When your heart can feel, you need no judgment to tell you the difference between one thing and another. You thus can begin to quit relying on your body's eyes to distinguish the true from the false, the real from the unreal.

21.4   Love appeals to you through the heart. God appeals to you through your heart. Your heart has not been open to the appeals of love partially because of your use of concepts. Concepts have been used to order your world and to assist your mind in keeping track of all that is in it. Your mind does not need this assistance. To begin to conceptualize in ways that touch your heart will free your mind of its reliance on thought concepts, thus allowing heart and mind to *speak the same language or to be communicated with in the same way.*

21.5   There has been a division between the language of your mind and heart. Your mind insists on thinking and learning in a certain way, a way contrary to the language of your heart, and so, like two people from different countries speaking different languages, there has been little communication and much misunderstanding. Occasionally the problems associated with a lack of a common language have been set aside when the actions needed in a certain circumstance have demanded cooperation. You see this in times of emergency or crisis of every kind. And like the two people from different countries who do not understand each other, working together momentarily diminishes the boundaries of language, and a temporary solidarity is formed through like action. At such times two strangers who are foreign to one another might recognize that the other's "heart is in the right place." The "right place" with two people — as with mind and heart — is the place of no division. The unification of mind and heart that produces right action currently occurs primarily in crisis situations because of a lack of shared language. The formation of a shared language can thus be seen to aid in unification.

The embrace can now be likened to the starting point of a   21.6
shared language, a language shared by mind and heart and by all people. It is a language of images and concepts that touch the one heart and serve the one mind.

Conflict between mind and heart occurs for an addi-   21.7
tional reason as well, although this conflict has at its root the problem of language as determined by perception. This is a problem of meaning. Mind and heart interpret meaning in different ways. You do not even begin to understand the enormity of this conflict or what it means to you, but I assure you that as long as mind and heart interpret meaning in different ways you will not find peace. You have, in the past, accepted these different interpretations as natural. You see that there are two ways of viewing a situation, even if you do not label one way of viewing or perceiving being of the mind and the other of the heart. And you *accept* the conflict of this dualism. You accept that your mind sees one truth and your heart another, and you act anyway! You act without agreement or resolution. You act without unity. And, just as if you were two people acting on different truths in the same situation, conflict cannot help but continue. No matter which path you follow, the path of the mind or the path of the heart, you will not get where you are wanting to go until they

are joined. You might imagine three paths — one path representing mind, one path representing heart, and one path representing wholeheartedness. The path of neither mind nor heart alone will take you where the path of unity will take you, and the journey will not be the same.

21.8 The major cause of the conflict that arises between mind and heart is the perception of internal and external differences in meaning. In extreme instances this is considered moral conflict, an example being the individual knowing the "right" thing to do but acting instead on what is the accepted thing to do within his or her community. In such an instance the external and internal meanings of the same situation are considered to be different. This is fairly easy to see in extreme circumstances, but it is a situation that exists constantly and in every instance until unity is achieved. Until unity is achieved you do not understand that you give meaning to all things, and that there is nothing and no one external to you who can determine meaning for you.

21.9 The final thing you must understand is that meaning does not change. While only you can determine meaning, and while only a wholehearted approach will determine true meaning, the truth is the truth and does not change. Only unity, however, allows you to see the truth and to claim it as your discovery and your truth as well as universal truth. Seeing the truth returns you to unity and to true communication or communion with your brothers and sisters in Christ. *Your brothers and sisters in Christ* is an expression that has always been meant to symbolize the unity of those who know the one truth.

21.10 Knowing the one truth is not about knowing a certain dogma or a set of facts. Those who know the truth do not see themselves as right and others as wrong. Those who know the truth find it for themselves by joining mind and heart. Those who know the truth become beings of love and light and see the same loving truth in all.

CHAPTER **22** | the INTERSECTION

cAs the universal becomes available, you will have no desire for the personal. Even so, you will find that what you consider your individuality or uniqueness is very much intact, but that it is different than you have always imagined it to be. You will find that you fulfill a grand purpose, and have a wonderful part to play in a grand design. You will not feel cheated by losing your separated self. You will feel free. — 22.23

We will talk much more of imagining now, and you may, at first, be resistant to this instruction. To imagine is too often associated with daydreaming, fiction, or make-believe, and these functions are all prescribed to be for certain parts of your life and for certain times that you deem appropriate. Please assure yourself, as I assure you, that now is an appropriate time, an essential time, for such activity. Your thoughts regarding imagining and imagination will change with your change in perspective on use. You will no longer be using your imagination but letting your imagination be of service to you. 22.1

We will be letting images serve as learning devices. They will enhance our use of language so that our language becomes one for both head and heart. We will begin by discussing the concept of *intersection* and look at it as a *passing through* that establishes a partnership or relationship. While we have previously discussed relationship as not being one thing or the other but a third something, we have not as yet discussed how this relationship is provided in form. Now we will do so. 22.2

22.3   A prime image of this idea is provided by the axis. A line passes through a circle and the circle revolves around the line, or axis. Imagine a globe spinning around its axis. You know that the globe is representative of the Earth. What you less frequently picture is the relationship between the globe and the axis, even though you realize the axis allows the globe to spin.

22.4   A second and equally worthy image is that of a needle passing through material. Of itself, it can hold two pieces of material together. With the addition of thread passed through the eye of the needle, it can bind many parts in many different configurations.

22.5   A needle can also pass through something like an onion, piercing many layers. While such a piercing has no intrinsic value in terms of purpose, it provides an image of a straight line passing through not one, but many layers of another substance.

22.6   Intersection is often seen as a division between rather than as a relationship among. The illustrations used here, however, concentrate upon a passing through rather than upon an idea of division, and they help to show that even what is divided by intersection remains whole.

22.7   The image of intersection is simply meant to represent the point where the world intersects with you — where your path crosses that of others, where you encounter situations in your daily life, where you experience those things that cause you to feel or believe in a certain way — and it is at this point of intersection that not only relationship, but partnership is found. The partnership of axis to globe, and of needle and thread to material, is easily seen. In these two examples, the partnership creates something that did not previously exist by providing a function and a purpose for each. In the case of the needle and the onion, partnership is less apparent because function and purpose are not apparent. Partnership is thus equated with productive intersection rather than intersection itself.

Meaning is similarly interpreted. Intersections that create function and purpose are deemed meaningful. Intersections that seem to have no function or purpose are deemed meaningless. The act of passing through is, of itself, seen as of little consequence. 22.8

Yet it is the passing through that creates the intersection. Everything within your world and your day must pass through you in order to gain reality. While you might think of this as everything outside of yourself, please, when thinking of this, use the words I have provided: *everything within your world.* In the act of passing through you assign meaning to everything within your world. The meaning you assign becomes the reality of the object you have assigned meaning to. You have seen your purpose as one of assigning meaning to that which intersects with you in a given way that you deem as purposeful. Yet it is in the passing through that meaning occurs of itself. 22.9

Further, it is the part of you through which everything within your world passes and your awareness of it that determines the meaning you give it. You are much more like unto the layers of the onion than the globe, with everything within your world needing to pass through layers with a seeming lack of purpose for the passing through. 22.10

You might think of the axis for a moment as a funnel through which eternity is poured and a whole heart as that which can allow free pass through of all that is provided. 22.11

22.12   In contrast, the layered approach to intersection causes you to feel as if external forces are bombarding you. These forces must pass through one or another of your five senses, which you might think of collectively as layers, and are allowed no other access. These forces must then be directed. Often great effort is expended keeping these forces from piercing your heart, the center of yourself. You instead deflect them, using your mind, which might be considered another layer, to send them to various compartments — or, continuing with the onion theme, to one of the various layers of yourself. These layers protect your heart, and a great percentage of them are involved with denial, with creating places where things enter and simply sit. These "things" are not really things, but are all that you have found no meaning for. Since your function is seen as assigning meaning rather than receiving meaning, that which you consider meaningless sits, and that which you consider beyond meaning sits. You might imagine yourself as the creator of an unfinished dictionary, and all that is sitting as that which you have determined you will, at some later date, get around to assigning meaning to.

22.13   The "meaningless" category might include such things as the happenings of your daily routine, chance encounters, illness, or accidents, while in the "beyond meaning" category exists the relationship that broke your heart, grief, poverty, war, the events that seemed to alter your destiny, the search for God. By using the word *sit,* I mean to imply that these things have not passed through you and in the act of passing through formed a relationship and a partnership with you.

22.14   While passing through would seem to imply an entry and exit point, the relationship developed during the pass through continues. Just as wind or water passing through an entry and exit point has an impact and a motion, so does what passes through you provide the movement of your journey. What passes through you is transformed by the relationship with you just as surely as you are transformed by the relationship with it.

When you remove yourself from the self-held position of "meaning giver," you let things be what they are and, allowed to be what they are, their meaning is naturally revealed. What this takes is a pass-through approach and a relinquishment of the idea of bringing things to a stop where they can be examined under a microscope quite apart from their relationship to you or to anything else.

22.15

Imagine yourself brought to such a halt and examined apart from everything else within your world. Anyone wanting to learn anything about you would be wiser to observe you as you are within your world. Would you still be the same person in a laboratory? Are you still who you are when another takes you into his or her mind and assigns meaning to you?

22.16

You have made of yourself a laboratory where you bring everything for examination, categorization, testing, and filing away. This is the scenario that separates you from everything else within your world. Everything has meaning only according to what it means to you and not as what it is.

22.17

Obviously two kinds of meaning are being talked about. The first we talked of earlier as the finding of truth. The second is what we are talking of here, the finding of a definition, a personal meaning. Can you see the difference?

22.18

The personal and individual is the "I" we are dispelling. Think a moment of how you tell a story or report on events that have taken place within your life. You personalize. You are likely to report on what a certain set of circumstances meant "to you." This kind of thinking is thinking with the

22.19

small "I." "I saw." "I felt." "I thought." "I did." The individual, personal, separated self is at the center of all such stories. One quite literally cannot conceive of the story without the "I." Yet this you must learn to do, and this task is given you as an exercise.

22.20   Begin to imagine life passing through you rather than getting stopped for examination at its intersection with you. Begin to imagine seeing the world without the emphasis on your personal self. Begin to form sentences and eventually to tell stories without the use of the "I" pronoun. This will seem, at first, as if it is depersonalizing the world and making it less intimate. It will seem as if you are shirking some primal responsibility to assign meaning to everything. Rather than resisting this, strive to cease giving meaning. Start quite simply. Go from the broad to the specific. For example, when you walk out your door in the morning you might generally think, *"What a lovely day."* What this sentence says is that you have immediately taken in your surroundings and judged them. It is a lovely day "to you." The day has all or most of the requirements you find pleasing in a day. Replace such a thought with: "The grass is green. The birds are singing. The sun is warm." Simple reporting.

22.21   When you are asked questions such as, "How was your day?" respond as much as possible without using the words *I* or *my.* Quit referring to people and things in terms of ownership, saying "my boss," "my husband," "my car."

22.22   This removal of the personal "I" is but a first step to returning you to the consciousness of unity, a first step in going beyond meaning as definition to meaning as truth. As odd and impersonal as it will seem at first, I assure you the feeling of impersonality will be replaced quickly with an intimacy with your surroundings that you never felt before.

This intimacy itself will allow you to see your "self" as an 22.23
integral part of all that exists within your world rather than
as the small and insignificant personal self you generally
accept as your "self." By eliminating the personal, the universal becomes available. As the universal becomes available,
you will have no desire for the personal. Even so, you will
find that what you consider your individuality or uniqueness
is very much intact, but that it is different than you have
always imagined it to be. You will find that you fulfill a grand
purpose, and have a wonderful part to play in a grand design.
You will not feel cheated by losing your separated self. You
will feel free.

23 | the FREEDOM
of the BODY

*Y*et *how can you become a
master of what another would teach? Of lessons
another would select? Your life must become your
teacher, and you its devoted pupil. Here is a curriculum designed specifically for you, a curriculum only
you can master.* — 23.29

Knowing and love are inseparable. When this is realized, it   23.1
is obvious that love is the only true wisdom, the only true
understanding, the only true knowing. Love is the great
teacher. And your loving relationships the means of learning
love.

The lessons learned from love will go a long way in assuag-   23.2
ing your remaining fears about the loss of individuality you
believe will accompany the loss of your separated self. For, as
each of you has found as you have loved another, the more
you love and long to possess a loved one, the more you realize that your loved one cannot be possessed. While in a love
relationship the greatest knowing is sought and, with willing
partners, attained; one's partner in such a relationship still
transcends complete knowing. The relationship becomes the
known. While it is your nature to seek for more, it is also
the nature of life to exist in relationship and to become
known through relationship. This is how knowing comes
to be. Knowing through relationship is not a "second best"
situation. It is how life is. It is how love is.

23.3   Thus, while your partner in love transcends total knowing, this too is "how it is." How it is meant to be. Love inviolate. Each of you is love inviolate. Yet relationally, you may be able to "read each other's thoughts," be cognizant of the slightest switch in mood, finish each other's sentences. You know the other would lay down his or her life for you, rise to any occasion of your need, share your every fear and joy.

23.4   Non-partnered love also shares a knowing through relationship. The loved one may be on the other side of the country, separated by distance, previous choices, or past hurts, and yet a relationship continues.

23.5   In both partnered and non-partnered love relationships, the one you come to know, the only one who does not transcend total knowing, is your Self.

23.6   The same is true of your relationship with God. As in any love relationship, the desire to know God can be all consuming. Yet, while God transcends knowing, your relationship with God is how you know both God and your Self.

23.7   Let me remind you of a key learning aid discussed some pages back: *You would not be other than you are.* No matter how much you grow to love another, that love does not cause you to want to *be* the other person. That love causes you to want to have a *relationship* with the other person. This should tell you something about the nature of love.

23.8   When obsessively in love you may want the other person to be *you,* but rarely the other way around. This is what has caused you to make God over in your own image and to try to do the same to others. This comes of seeing oneself as an image rather than as a being existing in relationship. This comes from ego rather than from the true Self.

What you long for is re-union. Yet reunion too is relation-ship, because union is relationship. Imagine a crowd of people in a small room. This is not relationship. When you are tempted to think of relationship having to do with phys-ical proximity, think of this example. Now imagine commu-nities of faith. Around the world, people are united in belief, and not only in religious beliefs. Ideology, politics, profes-sion unite people. "Parties" and "associations" are formed to foster the idea of unity through shared belief. They are not necessary, as is seen by the reality that they only form after the fact. The belief fosters the form and the form is then meant to foster the belief.   23.9

This is true of the body as well. Think of the way in which the word *body* is used and this will be clear. The *body* politic. A *body* of knowledge. Belief fostered the form and the form was meant to foster the belief. Thus belief and form have a symbiotic relationship. Understanding of this *loving* relationship can help you to experience freedom of the body, which is an extension, in form, of your belief in the personal "I."   23.10

Belief fosters union. Union does not foster belief, because in unity belief is no longer required. Belief fostered the union of atoms and cells into the form required by the belief in the separated self. Belief of another kind can foster the creation of form of another kind.   23.11

If form is an extension of belief you can see why what you believe is critical to how you live with form. We are speak-ing here of ways of thinking similar to those which you term induction and deduction. In the past, exercises have most often begun with an alteration of beliefs regarding form. Here we have taken an opposite approach, beginning with exercises to alter your belief in your identity and concluding   23.12

with exercises to alter your belief in form. This is consistent with our primary focus on learning from the heart. The mind goes from the small to the large, the heart from the large to the small. Only the wholehearted see the connection of all.

23.13 I repeat: *Belief of another kind can foster the creation of form of another kind.* A wholehearted belief in the truth about your Self is what is required to cause this to be so. It is what is necessary now. It will change the world.

23.14 *Belief of another kind* is what miracles are all about. It is what you are all about as a miracle worker. For you to change your beliefs is the miracle that we are after, the result we seek from this Course.

23.15 Obviously, your belief in who and what you are is the basis for your entire foundation, a foundation previously built on fear. Clearly, belief in the body was easily translated into a belief in the validity of fear. When you are free of this misperception, this inaccurate belief, your body will be freed. It will no longer be an object of use but a means of service.

23.16 Freeing your perception from your nearly immutable belief in form will allow for all changes in form required by the miracle. Form is not a constant but a result. While you believe belief is the result of form, it is not. Form is the result of belief. Thus belief is not only capable of changing form but also is necessary in order to do so.

23.17 History has shown you that what you believe is possible becomes possible. Science has proven the link between researcher and research findings. Still you find it difficult to believe that what is possible depends upon what you can imagine being possible. You must cease to see the difficulty and begin to see the ease with which what you can imagine becomes reality.

You have no capabilities that do not serve you, because they were created to serve you. The ability to imagine is such a capability, freely and equally given to all. Imagination is linked to true vision, for it exercises the combined capabilities of mind and heart. It is akin to perception, and can lead the way in changing how you perceive of yourself and the world around you. 23.18

Beyond imagination is the spark that allows you to conceive of what never was conceived of before. This spark is inspiration, the infusion of spirit. Taking the creation of form backwards, it leads to this conclusion: Spirit precedes inspiration, inspiration precedes imagination, imagination precedes belief, and belief precedes form. 23.19

Spirit is your more direct link with the one Source. Spirit is directly from the Source, while form is a by-product of spirit. Thus form is once removed, or further away from the Source. Again working backwards, however, the form you have created is still a step necessary in the return to the Source. The necessary step is that of moving beyond form — recognizing and acknowledging form for what it is and then continuing on, working backwards to change your belief, to allow imagination to serve you and spirit to fill you. 23.20

You then can move forward again, taking form beyond its given parameters and becoming a miracle worker. 23.21

The body encompasses or holds the belief. It is the composite of your beliefs, the totality. It will continue to hold former beliefs as well as new beliefs until old beliefs are purged. 23.22

The purging of old beliefs frees space for the new. It allows your form to reflect what and who you are now in terms that coincide with the "you" whom you have always been.

23.23   There is no quick route to this purging, as it is the most individual of accomplishments. As you learned your beliefs, you must unlearn your beliefs. As you begin the process of unlearning you may feel tested. You are not being tested but given opportunities for unlearning. To learn that a previously held belief is no longer valid is the only way to truly purge that belief.

23.24   These learning opportunities call for a period of engagement with life. Many of you will have begun to experience unlearning opportunities even while your study of this Course may have led you to turn inward and attempt to disengage from life. A period of engagement with life cannot be avoided, however, and your attempts to avoid it will only cause an increase in feelings generated by experiences of duality. While you hold conflicting beliefs within you, you will be conflicted and affected by polarity. Unlearning allows you to purge old beliefs so that only one set of beliefs is operative within you. This is the only route to the certainty you seek, and leads to true conviction. True conviction cannot be attained without this experience of unlearning and purging.

23.25   All unlearning opportunities are opportunities for miracle readiness. There is no trick to identifying unlearning opportunities. From this point forward, I assure you, all experiences will be thus until unlearning is no longer needed. If you will remember that the one exercise for your mind is dedicating all thought to union, you will keep your mind engaged and less resistant to unlearning. When you feel resistance — and of course your mind will resist unlearning what it has striven to learn — return your dedication to union. Acknowledge your mind's resistance as a sign that unlearning is going on. Acknowledge it but do not engage it.

What will happen when you look at each situation as a chal- 23.26
lenge to your beliefs? If you do not remember that you are involved in a process of unlearning that will lead to the conviction you have so long sought, you will indeed feel tested and will try to take control of the learning situation. Not taking control, however, is the key to unlearning. What you term as *being in control* is simply another way of saying *acting on old beliefs*. As long as you attempt to remain in control, old beliefs will not be purged.

Attempting to exert control over learning situations is a 23.27
reflection of belief that you have nothing to learn. An attitude of openness is required for unlearning and new learning both. Control opposes openness. Mastery comes through the process of both unlearning and learning anew. This is but another way of stating that which was stated in *A Course in Miracles:* Resign as your own teacher. The desire to control is the desire to remain your own teacher and/or to choose your teachers and learning situations. Neither can occur if you would truly choose to change your beliefs and move on to the new or the truth.

Looked at in another way, this process has much in common 23.28
with forgiveness. The action associated with it raises it to a level similar to that of atonement. It is an undoing accompanied by a new means of doing. In the process of unlearning, both forgiveness and atonement occur. You recognize that your false beliefs were the result of faulty learning. As unlearning is replaced by new learning, judgment falls away as your innocence is established. Can a child be found guilty when the child has not yet learned that which is needed for right action?

23.29 You might ask, how do you learn what you have failed to learn previously? What are the lessons? What is the curriculum? How will you know when you have achieved a learning objective? Yet how can you become a master of what another would teach? Of lessons another would select? Your life must become your teacher, and you its devoted pupil. Here is a curriculum designed specifically for you, a curriculum only you can master. Only your own life experiences have led to the learning you have accumulated and translated into beliefs. Only your own life experiences will reverse the process.

The time of tenderness precedes the time of peace and is the forerunner of compassion. The time of tenderness is thus the final learning ground before accomplishment is complete. The learning that occurs during the time of tenderness is learning from love. — 24.4

Where you learned to hate, you will learn to love. Where you learned to fear, you will learn safety. Where you learned to distrust, you will learn trust. And each learning experience will be a learning experience *because* it will touch your heart. It may be as simple as a smile from a child that melts away all the resentment you held from your childhood — *because* you allow that smile to touch your heart. It may be a time of weepiness and what you would term emotionalism. You may feel as if everything makes you want to cry because everything will touch you, each lesson will feel tender. Unlearning has no harshness about it. If you simply allow it to come, it will reward you constantly with what can best be described as tenderness. 24.1

The time to resist tenderness is over. The time to resist the tears of weariness is over. This is the time of the embrace. 24.2

These feelings of tenderness can be seen as a sign. Let them alert you that unlearning is taking place. Welcome them as harbingers of this good news. Know that the time of tenderness is a sure path on the way home. 24.3

24.4   The time of tenderness precedes the time of peace and is the forerunner of compassion. The time of tenderness is thus the final learning ground before accomplishment is complete. The learning that occurs during the time of tenderness is learning from love. No lessons learned without love touch your heart. No lessons that do not touch your heart will accomplish anything. The purpose of the final lessons is both unlearning and moving through unlearning to new learning. These lessons must be accomplished in life and require an engagement with life. This engagement is a promise, a commitment. It requires participation, involvement, attention, being present. These are the lessons with which we will conclude.

25 DEVOTION as a TYPE of PARTICIPATION

You begin to live from love when the personal self gets out of the way. And when the personal self gets out of the way in any instance, it is the turning point. It is the signal that you are ready to live from love. This is what this Course is about. Living from love. — 25.16

To devote oneself to an objective is a vow to accomplish. To be devoted is to be prayerful. As we said in the beginning, to pray is to ask for all to be included in what you do. Devotion is thus our first lesson in learning how to be engaged in life during the time of tenderness. 25.1

Devotion is the outcome of love and in this instance is an action word, a verb, a means of serving and being served by love. Devotion is a particular type of participation. It cannot be faked. But it can be practiced. 25.2

You, dear children, have faked your way through much of life. You have faked confidence when you are uncertain, interest where you feel indifference, knowledge of things about which you know nothing. But those who have tried to fake love cannot do it. The same is true of devotion, because there is no real devotion without love. 25.3

Love cannot be faked because you know love. Because you know it, imitations of love are immediately felt. You may 25.4

choose to deny the feeling, but you cannot prevent it from occurring. You can attempt to earn the love of those from whom you desire it, you can attempt to buy it, change for it, or capture it. This you cannot do. Yet, love is always present. Let us spend a moment considering this contradiction.

25.5   How can love always be present when you can undeniably feel each and every absence of love? The problem is in the perceiver rather than the perceived. Each time you feel a lack of love, it comes from within yourself. This lack of love, or "faked" love of which you cannot help but be aware, is a signal to you that you want something. When you become aware that you want something, you are also becoming aware that you feel you lack something. All feelings of lack are synonymous with feelings of fear. Where there is fear, love is hidden. Love is rejected when a choice for fear is made. You cannot be without love, but you can reject love. When you reject love, it is hidden from you, because receiving completes giving. Each of your brothers and sisters are love inviolate. What each gives is incomplete until it is received.

25.6   When you feel a lack of love in others, you have projected your fear onto them. Only when you cease to do this will you feel true devotion.

25.7   When you feel lack of love, you feel as if the "other" gives you nothing. Yet it is your lack of ability to receive that causes this feeling. The practice of devotion is a means by which you can purify your engagement with life and all you encounter within it. Devotion is synonymous with true service. True service does not look for what another has to give or what another has that you might use. True service recognizes God's law of giving and receiving, and the practice of devotion is, in effect, the practice of allowing giving and receiving to be one. It is, during the time of tenderness, a true practice that, like vigilance, is a means to a desired end. You must practice recognizing your feelings of lack of love, and realize these feelings come from your inability to receive. Do this practice until it is no longer needed.

Devotion is inclusive. It implies a subject and an object: One who is devoted and one who is an object of devotion. While we are moving away from subject/object relationships to the relationship of unity, the idea of one who is devoted, and of those for whom devotion is practiced, is useful during the time of tenderness. It will lead to the understanding of oneness as completion, an understanding of giving and receiving as one.   25.8

Devotion leads to harmony through action. This is possible for you now only if you have integrated the most basic teaching of this Course and no longer feel duped by life. All of your contests of will are supported by your contention that you have been misled. It is as if you have paid for your ticket, arrived for the concert, and been told your ticket is not valid. This makes you angry. This anger is reenacted in thousands of different scenarios in your life day after day and year after year until you realize and truly believe the basic tenets this Course has put forward.   25.9

To be in concert, just as to perform a concert, is contingent on harmony. It is being in agreement about the purpose for which you are here and your entitlement to be fully present here. If you still believe you are here to acquire some perceived ideal separated state, then all action will be out of harmony. If, however, you have accepted the basic tenets of this Course and believe you are here to realize unity, then all action will be in harmony. If you believe you and your brothers and sisters are here in a state of reprisal, having fallen from grace, then all action will be out of harmony. If you believe you and all other living things are here in a state of grace,   25.10

then all action will be in harmony. If you believe one living thing is more important than any other, then all action will be out of harmony. If you believe all are essential, then all action will be in harmony.

25.11   While one special relationship continues, all special relationships continue because they are given validity. The holy relationship of unity depends on the release of the beliefs that foster special relationships.

25.12   To believe you are in concert with the universe is to believe that you have no need for struggle, to believe you have no lack, to believe in your state of grace. While you believe even one person is against you, you are not in concert with God. While you believe fate works against you, you are not in concert with the universe. These attitudes confirm a continuing belief in your separated and vulnerable state. During the time of tenderness, you will learn, through the practice of devotion, to identify and reject all such attitudes and to adopt an attitude of invulnerability.

25.13   An attitude of invulnerability is necessary now. It is not arrogance or a means by which to flirt with risk and danger. It is simply your reality. During the time of tenderness you may feel vulnerable. But the time of tenderness is a time of healing, and as you are healed you will realize you are no longer vulnerable to being wounded. Fear of being wounded — physically, mentally, emotionally, and spiritually — has kept you from engaging with life. Being healed and recognizing your own state of being healed is a key purpose of the time of tenderness. You cannot realize your true identity while you hang on to wounds of any kind. All wounds are evidence of your belief that you can be attacked and hurt. You have not necessarily seen disappointment as attack or hopelessness as hurt, but you do feel these emotions as wounds. While you think you can remain disappointed or disillusioned, you will not be invulnerable. There is always, behind every disappointment or disillusion, every attack and every hurt, a person you believe acted toward you without love. While you believe feelings of lack of love come from anywhere but within, you will not be invulnerable.

A realization of your invulnerability is not necessary in terms of use but in terms of service. Those who claim invulnerability and use it as a test of fate, or an excuse to challenge the mighty forces of humanity or nature, will eventually lose the game they play. True invulnerability can only be claimed by those who recognize it as part of their true identity. Invulnerability will then serve you and your brothers and sisters. Its service is one of conquering fear and allowing love to reign. 25.14

Involvement flows from participation and engagement. While it may conjure up notions of joining movements or parties, or of making social contributions, pure joining is its objective. The first joining comes from within and it is putting into practice the lessons of joining mind and heart in wholeheartedness. 25.15

This first joining is a choice made from love without regard for the personal self. You begin to live from love when the personal self gets out of the way. And when the personal self gets out of the way in any instance, it is the turning point. It is the signal that you are ready to live from love. This is what this Course is about. Living from love. Living from love is what will reverse the lessons of the past. Reversing the lessons of the past is what will allow you to live in love in every instance. 25.16

Living in love in every instance is what occurs when the whole Self is involved in the love of life. There are no "parts" 25.17

of the Self fractioned off and holding resentments. There are no "parts" of Self living in the past or the future. There is not a "mindful" Self living separately from a "soulful" Self. There is not a "worker" Self living separately from a "prayerful" Self. All Selves are joined in wholeheartedness. The one Self is solely involved in living love.

25.18   As you begin to live love, a reverse of what you might expect to happen will happen. While you may expect that everything will take on greater importance, the reverse will at first be true. You will see little in what you do that matters. You will wonder why you are unconcerned about many of the things you have been concerned about previously. Your life may actually seem to have less purpose. You may begin to wonder what to do. You will almost certainly question what you do for a "living." You will question many patterns and habits.

25.19   This is unlearning taking place. It may feel frustrating and be tinged with anxiety, anger, confusion, perplexity, even rage. You will doubt that these are the proper feelings of a person living love. Yet they are common feelings of unlearning, and should be accepted as such. You will learn that while some things you have done and will continue to do may not matter, they may still be done with patience, grace, and love. You will learn that other things you have done, beliefs you have held, patterns and habits that have occupied you, will not accompany you into your life of love. These you will leave behind.

25.20   You may also notice a growth in your desire to take credit for what you have created, and a desire to create anew. At this stage, this desire will come from a feeling of needing to reassert the self. This need will arise as you realize that you can take no credit for your life. Wanting to take credit is of the ego, and at this stage the desire to create may be linked with ego as well. Your personal self will be looking for a place in which to reside. It will be looking for identity. It will want to say: *"This is who I am."* This is an exciting sign, for it means the old identity is losing hold. Be patient during this time, and your new identity will emerge. If the urge to create is strong, certainly let it serve you. But do not seek for praise or acknowledgment of your creations at this time. You will soon realize that creation is not of, or for, the personal self.

This will be a time of discernment. You may feel it as a time   25.21
of decision making, but the less you attempt to make conscious decisions the quicker your unlearning will take place and the lessons of discernment occur. Discernment is needed only until you are better able to comprehend the whole. Comprehension of the whole is aided by a return to wholeness of the Self. Until wholeness of the Self is complete, discernment is necessary.

Practice discernment by being still and awaiting wisdom. Your   25.22
feeling of being identity-less will make decision making and choices of all kinds appear to be difficult during this time. You must realize decisions and choices are made by relying upon the very lessons you are in the process of unlearning. At the same time, however, decisions and choices will seem to need to be made with increasing frequency. Your feeling of needing to make new choices, while strong, will not necessarily reflect real need but rather an impatience with the way things are and were. You will want to force change rather than wait for it to arrive. If you acknowledge your impatience as a sign of readiness for change that does not necessarily require action on your part, you will feel some relief.

When action is seen to be necessary, this is exactly when a   25.23
time of stillness is needed. You might think of this time of

stillness as a time of consulting with your new identity. Simply sitting quietly, and posing the question or concern that is in need of appropriate action will suffice. When an answer comes to you, acknowledge that it is an answer from your new identity and express appreciation for it. While you will at times doubt that you have received an answer or that the answer you have received is correct, you will soon learn to trust this quiet process of discernment. You will know you have succeeded when you truly feel as if you have "turned the question or concern over" and allowed it to be responded to in a new way.

25.24 When you are guided to act in ways that are contrary to usual patterns of action you have taken in the past, you will often meet resistance. Try to be lighthearted at such times and to remember that if it "doesn't matter," you might as well try the new way. Remind yourself that you have nothing to lose. You will soon learn that this is so. You will also soon realize why this time of engagement with life is necessary. Experience is necessary to complete the cycle of unlearning and learning.

25.25 Being fully engaged with life while taking the time for discernment is uncommon. Putting action before stillness, activity before rest, is seen as synonymous with a full life. We must, therefore, speak a bit of what a full life is.

This is the invitation to the celebration. This is the invitation to greet this day with no worry, disappointment, or planning. This is the invitation to greet your Self and to find your Self within this day. — 26.18

It is often spoken of with some amazement that I lived a short life, preached for only a small part of it, traveled not very far, had few possessions or influential friends. We have talked before of the tragedy you feel when anyone dies young. You each have some notion of what you believe a full life to be. For some of you it would include marriage and children, for others career, religious commitment, or creative endeavors. Some would think of travel and adventure, friendships, or financial security. Most of you will think of having a long life.

26.1

Many of you question the line between fate and accomplishment. Are some chosen for greatness? Others for mediocrity?

26.2

Few recognize the tragedy in the *life* of a person, except in instances of great dichotomy, perhaps best expressed in the life of the tragic hero. This observance of tragedy *in life* occurs only when the observation is also made of the greatness, the glory, *in the life*. Without the recognition of the glory of life, there is no recognition of tragedy until the life

26.3

has ended. In contrast, in the life of the tragic hero, excluding those who are posthumously given such a title, the tragedy is most often considered a fall from greatness. It is seen in the allure of myths where those who associate themselves too closely with the gods are punished for such folly. Such fear of greatness and glory, of the possibility of a fall from greatness and glory, results in many tragedy-less lives. "Nothing ventured, nothing gained," is an axiom for such lives. Fear of the "fall" is a primal fear, the first fear, the fear behind all such axioms.

26.4   Again I offer my life as the example life and reiterate the message expressed in *A Course in Miracles:* The true meaning of the crucifixion is that it was the last and final end to all such fears and myths. All such fears were taken to the cross with me and banished in the resurrection of the glory that is ours.

26.5   Do not be afraid. My brothers and sisters in Christ, realize that there is no cause for fear. You cannot fly too closely to the sun. You cannot be deceived any longer by tales of woe or of fallen heroes. Your story is one of glory. Your greatness can no longer be denied, unless *you* deny it.

26.6   Do you feel beautiful and prized and worthy? Then so shall you be.

26.7   No fear is greater than the fear of meaninglessness. And, as stated before, the quest for meaning is how you have described your purpose here. To have no meaning to attach to your life is the tragedy you see within it and attempt to keep hidden from yourself. This fear goes hand in hand with your fear of the fall, for if you were to attempt to assign the meaning to your life that you think it should have, a fall would surely await you, at least in your imaginings. You are thus caught in a double bind, living a life you feel is devoid of meaning and letting fear keep you from seeking the meaning you would give it. You feel no inherent sense of purpose, no grace, no meaning beyond what you would give to your own endeavors.

This is what we now leave behind as we seek to become involved with life. I say *we* because I am with you and will not leave your side. I say *we* because your first involvement is involvement with Christ, an involvement that links us in oneness and glory once again. I say *we* because *we are* life. I say *we* because we cannot live love apart from one another. 26.8

You do not yet, but will soon realize the happiness that is ours. Your mind can just not accept that happiness as well as meaning is due you through no effort of your own. Scenes of your life play through your mind that "prove" that you are neither inherently happy, nor your life inherently meaningful. Your reliance on these scenes and memories must be broken before my words can reach your mind and begin to replace these scenes with new ones. Until that time is upon you, let my words touch your heart. 26.9

You who struggle to understand what these words say and what they might mean, who strive to find the clues to what they ask you to do, will find it difficult to cease your struggle and your striving. You find it almost impossible still to believe effort is not called for — that what your heart but wishes for could simply come true through your acceptance of these words. But I am prepared to make it easy for you. 26.10

You who have so sought happiness without finding it, rejoice. It is not lost. It does not require you to define it or put a name to it before it can be yours. Is this not what you have cried about in frustration? Have you not long sought to 26.11

put a name on happiness? Have you not long lamented that if you knew what would bring you happiness you would surely pursue it? Have you not long stated that if you knew what would bring meaning to your life you would surely do it? Have you not long wished to know your purpose? To be given a goal that would fulfill the longing in you? Have you not prayed for signs? Read books that have promised you a series of steps to take to get where you want to go, only to realize you know not where that is?

26.12   And have you not become impatient with advice, with teachers and with courses of study? Have you not felt at the limit of your patience with instruction? Have you not felt the call to live growing stronger in you by the day? Are you not anxious to say: *"Tell me what to do and I will do it"*? Are you not ready for certainty above all else? Are you not ready to be done with studying and to begin with living? Have you not become increasingly convinced that you have *not* been living, and wondered what it is you have been doing? Have you not grown weary of what passes for life in your world? Have you not wished you could throw out all the thoughts and worries that fill your mind and begin anew?

26.13   Are you not simply ready to be done with the way things have been and to begin a new way? Are you not ready to listen to a new voice?

26.14   All this frustration and impatience has been building. This buildup has been necessary. Now, like an explosion waiting to happen, it only needs a trigger to be released. With its release the new can begin.

26.15   This Course is but a trigger. These words the prelude to the explosion. It is as if you have been waiting for someone to whisper: *Now!* The whisper has come. The time is now.

Can you let the worries of today leave your mind? Can you let the disappointments of yesterday go and be no more? Can you let the planning for the future cease? Can you be still and know your Self?   26.16

This is perhaps disappointing to you, but it is all that is required. If you could truly succeed at doing this for one instant, you would experience all that is holy and be forever new.   26.17

You may experience disappointment at these words, and feel as if you have been waiting to be invited to a party and that the invitation hasn't come. This is because you are ready for the next step, the step of being engaged with life. The step of living from love. And I assure you, there is no need to sit about and wait for the time of the celebration to come. This is the invitation to the celebration. This is the invitation to greet this day with no worry, disappointment, or planning. This is the invitation to greet your Self and to find your Self within this day.   26.18

It requires no new plans. It asks not that you make any decisions. It asks not that you *do* anything new. This is an invitation from love to love. It asks only that you be open and allow giving and receiving as one to take place. It asks only that you be unoccupied with the old so that the new may arrive. It asks only that you listen to your heart and let your Self be heard.   26.19

I cannot tell you here what you will hear. How can I, when each of you will hear the answer of your heart? The calling of love to love inviolate? The answer that only you can hear. There is no mold, no form, no stock answer. This is why all answers have disappointed you in the past. Your answer is not the same as any other. No matter how filled with wisdom one person's answer may be, it is not yours.   26.20

26.21   You are a thought of God. An idea. This thought, or idea, is what you seek. It can be found only at its Source. Its Source is love, and its location is your own heart.

26.22   Think a moment of a novel or movie with no plot. This would be the same as saying that there was no idea brought to completion within the pages or in the film. In God's idea of you is all that is known about you. God's idea of you is perfect, and until now your form has been but an imperfect representation of God's idea. In God's idea of you is the pattern of the universe, much as within a novel, movie, piece of music, invention, or artistic idea is the completion of the pattern that will make that idea a masterpiece. An idea is irrevocably linked with its source and one with its source. Thus, there was no God separate from you to have this idea of you. You were birthed in unison with God's idea of you.

26.23   This does not need to be understood, but only accepted to the extent you can accept it. This is necessary because of your reliance on a God who is "other" than you for the provision of your answers. Acceptance of your birth in unison with God's idea of you is acceptance of your Self as co-creator of the pattern of the universe, acceptance of the idea or the story that is you. Can you not see that you were birthed into a place in the pattern of God's creation? Or that you not only can know but have always known of this place?

26.24   This is not a place of physical form but a place of holiness, an integral place in the pattern that is oneness with God. It is a place you have never left but that you long for, believing that you know it not. Your life here is much like a search for your story. Where will this chapter lead? What will the end be like? Was one event a mistake and another a blessing in disguise? You seek to know your story's table of contents, or at least a brief outline. Where does your life fit in the larger picture? And yet, you realize that — like reading a story — when the end is reached and all is known, the story is over except in memory and reflection and perhaps in speculation. What might a sequel reveal?

This viewing of your life as a story is what you do. You spend each day in review or speculation. What has happened and what will happen next? You attempt to rewrite previous chapters and to cast all the parts and plan all the events of the next. This is, in effect, your attempt to control what you do not believe you created, and what you feel deprived of creating. As a being birthed by a thought of God, you grew simultaneously with God's thought. You knew your place in the pattern of creation from the outset. A full life is quite simply a fulfillment of that thought and that pattern. The only way to know it is to think it once again. The only way to think it once again is to be whole-hearted, for a split mind and heart do not think clearly. 26.25

Being whole is being present. Being whole is being all you are. Being whole is being present as all you are. When this occurs you are All in All, One in being with your Father. 26.26

I fulfilled my story, my pattern, the idea of me that came from the thought of God. In doing so, I restored unity, one-ness with God. I ushered in the new way that you are now longing to adopt. I ushered in a time of being. 26.27

27 | BEING

*Y**our* being *here is not futile*
or without purpose. Your being *is itself all purpose, all*
honor, all glory. There is no being apart from being.
There is no being alive *and being* dead, *being* human
or being divine. *There is only being. Being is.* — 27.2

We return now to what your being is. Being is. As love is. You   27.1
have attached being to being *human.* In your quest to identify yourself, you simply narrowed yourself to the visible and
describable. Thus you have identified death as the only
means by which to reach oneness with your Father, knowing
that such oneness is not compatible with the human nature
you ascribe to yourself. In this one error do all errors lie. For
what quest can be fulfilled when the only answer to life seems
to be death? This is why and how my death and resurrection
provided an answer and an end to the need for answers.

Your *being* here is not futile or without purpose. Your *being*   27.2
is itself all purpose, all honor, all glory. There is no being
apart from being. There is no being *alive* and being *dead,*
being *human* or being *divine.* There is only being. Being is.

Yet being, like love, *is* in relationship. Thus, your purpose   27.3
here, rather than being one of finding meaning, is one of
coming to know through relationship. It is in coming to
know through relationship that you come to know your Self.

27.4   The purpose of this Course has been stated in many ways and is stated again here: The purpose of this Course is to establish your identity. The importance of this purpose cannot be underestimated. Let us address the question of why this is so important.

27.5   You have been caught in a cycle of seeing the self as important for a period of time and then seeing the self as unimportant for a period of time. Seeing the self as important seems at one time like a function of the ego, and at another as a function of the divine. You become confused between the personal self and a true Self only because you have not as yet identified your true Self. Once you have identified your true Self all such confusion will end.

27.6   We have already stated that relationship is the only "known" in an unknowable world. We have already stated that the only being who is not beyond the limits of total knowing is the Self. Thus it is in knowing the Self that all is known.

27.7   When you fully realize that the only way to know the Self is through relationship, your concerns about concentration on the self will end. Life is not a matter of self versus other. Life is a matter of relationship. Life is not a matter of human versus divine, but a matter of relationship between the human and the divine. Life is not a matter of one living thing versus another, but of the relationship between all living things.

27.8   If you can only come to know your Self through relationship, you can only come to know God through relationship. Christ *is* the holy relationship that exists between all and God, providing the bridge that spans the very concept of *between* and provides for the connection of unity. Thus your relationship with Christ always was and always will be. Your task here is to come to know that relationship once again.

The thought of God by which you were created is synony-   27.9
mous with the Christ in you. It is your relationship with
your Source and all that He created.

Can you begin to visualize or perceive your true identity as   27.10
relationship itself? And what of God? Can you unlearn all
concepts and free your mind to accept all relationship
instead? If all meaning and all truth lies in relationship, can
you be other than relationship itself? Can God? Can you
imagine relationship rather than singular objects and bodies,
as *all* that exists, and thus who you are and who God is? Is
it such a huge leap to go from saying you only exist in relationship to you only exist *as* relationship? You think it is,
and feel your self further diminished and lacking in identity
just by contemplating such an idea. And so you must be
reassured of the Self you are.

This establishment of your identity that we seek to do here is   27.11
not just so that you can better understand your Self or your
world, or even so that you can bring Heaven to Earth.
Although these are complementary goals, as stated before,
these are goals that you cannot accomplish "on your own" or
with the concept you now hold of yourself. Just as you can
look about and see that no two bodies on this earth are
exactly the same, the Self you are is a unique Self. A Self of
relationship does not imply a Self that is the same as all the
rest. But it does imply a Self that is integral to all the rest. You
matter, and you matter as an interactive part of the relationship that is life. You are already accomplished as who you are.
All is accomplished in unity. In separation you merely strive
for all that is yours in relationship. Relationship *is* unity, and
relationship is your natural state. It is who you are.

Because you do not understand does not mean that you are   27.12
not learning the truth. You do not understand because you

think in terms of singularity rather than in terms of unity. This is why this Course has not concentrated on your thinking. Again you are bidden to turn to your heart for the truth that is hidden there yet waiting to be revealed. Your heart knows of unity and knows not any desire to be alone and separate. Your heart understands relationship as its Source of being. You are not separate from your Source.

27.13   Living in relationship is living in love and is living as who you are. Living in relationship is living in the present. How do you learn to move from living in separation to living in relationship?

27.14   To live in relationship is to accept all that is happening in the present as your present reality, and as a call to be in relationship with it. It is the willingness to set aside judgment so that you are not contemplating what "should" be happening rather than what *is* happening. It looks past perception of "others" to relationship and wholeness. To live in relationship is to live in harmony even with conflict. It is an understanding that if conflict arises in your present there is something to be learned from your relationship with conflict.

27.15   Living in relationship is living from your center, the heart of your Self. It is complete reliance on relationship itself rather than on the mind. Thus your actions reflect the proper response to the relationship that is occurring in the present rather than to your preconceived notions of others, the previous judgments your mind once made and relies upon out of habit, or your considerations of what the situation might mean to your future. It is not the individual "you" that dictates your responses to situations based on surface interpretations of what those situations entail. It is rather the you in and within the relationship that responds out of the knowledge gained through relationship.

How often have you, even with the best of intentions, not 27.16
known the proper response to make? You even wonder as
you pray whether you should pray for specific outcomes or
for God's Will to be done. You fear being a miracle worker
because you do not think that you will ever know what is
called for.

As you learn to live in relationship in the present, this con- 27.17
fusion will pass. Your relationship will guide you surely to
the proper response. I use the term "proper" here not as a
measure of judgment, but as an indication that there is a
way in which those who live in relationship become certain,
and their willingness to act unimpeded by uncertainty. All
uncertainty is fear. All fear is doubt about one's self. How
can you not know how to respond when doubt is gone and
certainty has come? How can certainty ever come without
an understanding of the relationship of all things?

Does an understanding of the relationship of all things mean 27.18
that you will have power that is not of this world? Will you
see the future and the past, be cognizant of destiny and of
fate? You do have power that is not of this world, but this
does not mean power as you see it here, the power of details
and the information of which you think when desiring or
fearing a fate of prophecy. The power we speak of is the
power of *knowing*.

How often have you known the "right" thing to do with- 27.19
out knowing the details of what came before and what was
to come? Sometimes you have acted on this knowing, and
at other times not. Living in relationship provides a constant knowing of this sort, a simple knowing of a *way*
things are meant to be. It is a knowing felt within the
heart for which there still will be no proof, but for which
there will be the certainty you heretofore have lacked. The

typical fears you have experienced in the past will not arise within this knowing.

27.20   How will you know when you have achieved the state of grace in which you were created, and that you are living in relationship? You will know by the certainty you feel. If you do not feel this certainty, what can you do?

27.21   You are ready now, and all that will prevent you from living a life of love is unwillingness to do so. There is only one remaining source of such unwillingness. Your willingness will now depend on whether or not you trust. Do you trust these words? Do you trust in God? Can you trust in your Self?

Where you are is where you are supposed to be. The path to follow to all changes will be shown to you if you will but be attentive. If you follow the way that is shown to you, all uncertainty will end.   — 28.13

We must speak about bearing witness to what you have learned. As this Course bears witness to the truth, thus must your lives bear witness. Lest this too be distorted, it must be discussed.   28.1

This is not a contest. Bearing witness has become a spectator sport and it is not meant to be thus. How, then, you might ask, is the truth brought to those still living in illusion?   28.2

Because inner knowing is both individual and collective, both personal and universal, this is the source of all proof. And so you believe coming together to share common testimony validates the proof of inner and collective knowing. You think shared beliefs amass, like a congregation around a pulpit, and even believe in a theory of mass that purports that when a certain magnitude of belief occurs, evolutionary steps are brought about. This, however, is not about evolutionary steps, and so a process intent upon bringing the collective to a fever pitch of belief through common testimony is not our aim.   28.3

28.4   Trust and bearing witness go together, as the validation sought through bearing witness is a symptom of distrust. Few are chosen to be prophets, and the plethora of testimony taking place is brought about by innocence more so than by wisdom. This sharing of personal testimony has reached its zenith and will no longer be as welcomed or appreciated, so even were the intent of this Course to bring testimony together in such a way as to cause an evolutionary step, it would not work. Thus we must concentrate on wisdom, the wisdom of the heart.

28.5   There is a trust that goes beyond proof, and beyond the need for any witnessing at all. This is the trust of knowing. Knowing is of the heart, and holds a consistency and certainty that the dawn of innocence does not contain. The dawn of innocence is but a recognition of the most common denominator of existence. As such, it is a beginning only, a true dawn that must, as the sun rises, give way to day and the brilliance and clarity of the wisdom of which we speak.

28.6   This daytime of your journey is approaching. It is the time for the sun to cut through the mists of dawn. It is the middle of the journey, a time of teaching and of learning both. It is the time of planting and of harvest that comes before the time of rest. It is the time of celebration that comes before the quiet and the settling of the dusk.

28.7   You would think of this as the time of work being done. This it is, but without the drudgery of time *spent.* It is your time to shine, to be a light to those who live in darkness.

28.8   And yet it is a time of great humility. Of wearing the face of Christ for all to see. For here is wisdom gained and shared.

28.9   Do you not see that any attempt to turn bearing witness into a convincing argument for your point of view, no matter what that point of view may be, makes what you have come to know pointless to you as well as to those you would convince? You think that when you are enlightened enough to know, you are also enlightened enough to know what to do with what you know. While you continue to think of a separation in terms of *doing* and of *knowing,* it is obvious this cannot be the case.

As the dawn is unrestrained in its bursting forth, so has been your time of innocence. Not so the approach of day as the sun slowly rises and as slowly sets. This is a time of being both guided and restrained. A time of realizing that you can *know* without knowing what to *do,* and that this is not a mistake. Many reach this stage and, not knowing what to do with what they know, begin to doubt their knowing. This is a human response to a knowing that is not human in origin. Knowing is alien to you, and that is why you seek validation. Each validation is seen and felt as a reward, a prize, a confirmation that you believe allows your conviction to grow. Because you believe it, this is, at first, quite true. But now it is no longer the time to rely on conviction that comes from the witnesses you find along your way. They serve a limited purpose for a limited time. Now is the time to step beyond the validation that witnesses can give you. When this step is not taken, gatherings of witnesses abound, and what they bear witness to stops short of what they would see.

28.10

Witnesses are for the mind and fall short of devotion, which is the natural response of those who know and worry not of what to do. This is a difficult stage as you feel obligated and inspired to act and yet awkward in your actions. We have spoken before of the desire to create that may arise as you begin to enter this stage of your journey. This is often compounded by a feeling of wondering what is next as you wait

28.11

in anticipation for a calling of some kind, so certain are you of an impending challenge to action, of some necessary form to be given to what you carry within.

28.12   Again, as when you feel the need to convince others of your belief, the need to give form to what is beyond form misses the point of what you have gained. You may be asking now, "Are you saying to do nothing?" At the thought of this you will be aghast and, what is more, bitterly disappointed. Again, as in the beginning, you seek a task to accomplish, forgetting that only you can be accomplished.

28.13   When one thinks, "There is so much to say," one forgets to listen. Be guided in your going out. Be restrained in what you say. Be attentive in your listening. Where you are is where you are supposed to be. The path to follow to all changes will be shown to you if you will but be attentive. If you follow the way that is shown to you, all uncertainty will end. Uncertainty is where difficulty lies. Certainty and ease as surely go together. There are no more decisions for you to make. There is only a call for a dedicated and devoted will, a will dedicated to the present moment, to those who are sent to you and to how you are guided to respond to them. One will be a teacher, another a student. The difference will be clear if you listen with your heart.

A split mind and heart can prevent you from utilizing the power of choice, but it cannot prevent you from claiming this choice as your own. Choose anew and let the power of heaven come together to seal the rift between your mind and heart, and make you whole once again. — 29.19

To attend is to be present and to be of service. This is the meaning of which we speak when we ask for a commitment to life that requires your attention. It is both a request for focus and readiness and a request for service that can only be given in the present by a mind and heart available to the requirements of the present. It is the appropriate attitude for the time of tenderness, as it is an attitude of ministry.

29.1

Your function cannot be known to you while you shy away from the idea of service. Whether you realize it or not, you associate service with subjugation, particularly the idea of service to a higher Will or higher Cause. Some of you associate it with a lack of free will, a lack of choice, a course that will lead you to a subservient stature. Others think of it in terms of charity, and continue to see a difference between those who would serve and those who would be served. Few of you have as yet integrated this Course's definition of service into your lives. But now you shall. For you cannot bring the learning you have done here into an

29.2

engagement with life and not realize the true meaning of service, or in contrast, the true meaning of use.

29.3 You who have so worried over what to do have both welcomed and feared the idea of some kind of service being required of you. There is no mystery to this, as the idea of service in your society is one of enforced duty, as exemplified by your military service. You have no notion, as did people of the past, of being of service to God. This is a symptom of the reign of the ego and its ability to both aggrandize your notion of yourself, and to minimize it. To be of service to God is not to be a slave to God but to attend to God. To give God your attention and your care. You who would cry, *God make use of me,* only need to give to God your devotion and your willingness to serve instead of use.

29.4 Further, you need to let the universe be of service to you rather than trying to use the universe to accomplish your goals. These adjustments in your attitude toward service will bring about the completion of the cycle of giving and receiving, and the beginning of wholeness.

29.5 This is as true for your own goal of wholeheartedness as it is for any wider goal of unity, for they are the same goal. Wholeheartedness is unity regained. Your return to unity is your return to your full power and your ability to be of quite literal service to God and your brothers and sisters.

29.6 If God were to speak to you Himself and tell you of what means your service would be to Him, He would but tell you this: *My child, return to me.* God has no Will apart from yours. Your return to unity is all God seeks for you, for Himself, and for all His children. The return to unity was my accomplishment, and all that is meant by what I have often repeated here: Only you can be accomplished. Your service is but dedication to this goal.

My return to unity accomplished this goal for all, for all are one in me and one in unity. This is why you have no need to concern yourself with anything other than this goal. Your realization of this goal's accomplishment is your realization of your divinity, a state unaltered and yet in need of your recognition and return. 29.7

While this goal may at first appear to be one of selfish intent and individual gain, it is not. A return to unity is a return to unity. From within the center, the core of unity, your accomplishment goes out to the world, as mine once did. 29.8

The time of tenderness is the time of your approach to unity. The atonement that is accomplished here is the means of opening the gate to your approach. No one has closed this gate to you, but you by your own hand pulled it shut as you departed your heavenly home, and you do not remember that your own hand can open it once again. It is a gate of illusion, of mist, of clouds before the sun. Your hand is outstretched now and your light is clearing away the mist. The gateway to unity stands before you, an arch of golden light beneath a rainbow vibrant with the colors of life. Life, not death, assures your approach. God Himself will guide your entry. 29.9

Many of you have noticed the consistency with which you have glorified falsely that which you would imitate from creation. In work too you will find an example of this. For you all know that work and service somehow go together. In many cultures has work thus been glorified and made to seem as if it is the proper use of a life. And yet, as your Father's child, your work is as his. Your work is that of creation. Your 29.10

creation is your service to the world as your Father's work is his service to you. As you cannot imagine God toiling, so you should cease to imagine yourself doing thus.

29.11 Many of you think of life itself as toil. There is much you need to do just to stay alive, and if a thing is required, expected, necessary, your tendency is to rebel against it and to seek for ease in getting it done or ways to avoid doing it at all. Thus have your paper plates and dishwashers taken the ritual from a meal, your mass manufacturing the satisfaction of the hand made. While this is neither good nor bad, this attitude of life as toil is part of your rebellion against ideas of service. You have no time for more than you do now, and you think of service, if you think of it at all, as something to be fit in here or there where it is convenient in your busy schedule.

29.12 It is extremely important for you to realize that God's work takes place outside of time, as do all acts of true service or creation. This is not a readily understandable concept, but one that is necessary for you to have faith in. It is essential to your release of the concept of toil and your acceptance of your function here.

29.13 No matter how busy your schedule, it is only a schedule in terms of your perception of it. Your *schedule* is just another way of saying *your life,* and an alternative view of how you look at your life, when seen thus, is absolutely necessary.

29.14 No wholeness will be possible for you while you look at life in terms of schedules, plans, time tables, or things to get done. No wholeness will be possible for you while you compartmentalize your life into designated pieces, giving yourself time for work and time for leisure and seeing them not as the same thing. Life is life. Life is. As love is.

Life is service to God. God is service to life. You are God in 29.15
life. Thus you are both life and service to life, both God and
service to God. All of the vast universe was created the same:
to live and to serve life, to be of God and be of service to
God. To be served and to serve. To be provided for and
to provide. To have needs met and to meet needs. This circular nature of the universe leaves no one unattended. Yet
you realize this not.

The separation but accentuated this manner of functioning 29.16
and made of it something difficult and challenging, something to be changed. The separation accentuated this manner of functioning and made of it, as of the rest of creation,
something that it is not. The separation accentuated this
manner of functioning, but it did not create it. Life exists in
service to itself. This could also be stated thus: Life exists
in relationship. Relationship is the interaction within which
service occurs. The replacement of the idea of service with
the idea of use made for the existence of special relationships. The idea of use created all ideas of toil as the only
means of having needs met. The idea of use created all
notions of distrust, starting with — as we have stated before
— your ideas of using the very body you call your home
rather than allowing it to serve you.

The universe exists in reciprocal relationship or holy rela- 29.17
tionship, rather than special relationship. This is the nature
of existence, as unity is the nature of existence and cannot
be changed and has not changed, although you believe it
not. It is a joyful relationship, as the nature of relationship is
joy. Once you have given up your belief in separation this
will be known to you.

The choice to change your belief is before you. Are you not 29.18
ready to make it? As you once chose separation you can now

choose unity. Not knowing that unity was a choice prevented you from making this choice before now. Now I tell you clearly, the choice is yours. Choose once again.

29.19　As you make your choice, remember your choice must be wholehearted, for it is in wholeheartedness that the power of choice exists. A split mind and heart can prevent you from utilizing the power of choice, but it cannot prevent you from claiming this choice as your own. Choose anew and let the power of heaven come together to seal the rift between your mind and heart, and make you whole once again.

29.20　Claiming your identity and your power to make choices is an act that comes from an entirely different place than decision making. Claiming is akin to prayer and is but an asking, an asking for your true inheritance. You have felt that you need to know for what it is you ask. And yet you cannot know until you inherit. Can you have faith that your true inheritance is what you truly desire, even knowing not exactly what that inheritance is? Can you not follow me in my choice and accept it as your own?

29.21　You who have so long been afraid to claim your smallest gifts, look again at claiming with the definition I have provided. Claiming is also contrary to how you have perceived of it in terms of claiming something for your own: You claim not to own or to separate what you have from what another has and then to call it special. You claim in order to reclaim your Self.

29.22　How can one's talent cause another to be less talented? How can one's service deprive anyone else of the right to serve? No two are alike. Only in God are all the same.

29.23　This is the great divide, the separation, between the visible and the invisible, the indivisible and the divisible. Only those reunited with God achieve the state of unity. Only the state of unity exists.

Your gifts, your talents, your uniqueness, are your service. 29.24
Can you not look at them thus? And can you not come to understand the reciprocal nature of giftedness? That what God has given only needs to be received? That what you have received only needs to be given? The indivisibleness of God is simply this: an unbroken chain of giving and receiving. Thus is this a definition of unity as well.

Service is but another way of stating this law of creation, this 29.25
unbroken chain of giving and receiving. All your worry over the future and the past is but a worry about the return of gifts given. What gift of opportunity did you not accept in the past, might you not recognize in the future? What gift of fortune, what chance encounter, what decision might have changed your life? What should you have done that you didn't do? What might you do in the future if not for your fear of where the direction you choose might take you? What peace might you know if you realized, truly realized, that all gifts come but once and are forever? The past nor the future matter not. All is available in the here and now where giving and receiving occur.

No chance to learn or grow is ever missed. Each still exists, 29.26
though not in time. Each still exists, but in the present. Can you replace your attention to the past and future with an attention to the present?

We, all of us together, are the heartbeat of the world. Without unity we would not be. Without our Source, which is God, we would not be.

— 30.13

How is being *present* different than *being?* Are they not the same thing? Should they not be? And yet how seldom are you fully present for your own life, your own Self, your own being. If you were fully aware of your own being, you would be in oneness with your Father.   30.1

How can one be distracted from oneself? And yet you are.   30.2
Many go through life searching for self-definition, self-actualization. Where are they as they search? Where is their being? If reaching a particular destination is all that is sought, the journey becomes but the means for getting there. All learning is seen as preparation for the future, or for some eventual outcome, rather than for your being. You thus attempt to learn for something other than your Self, for some purpose other than your Self. Thus was service given another route for being separated from the Self and your function here. When you learn in order to contribute something to your work and your world, you bypass your Self.

30.3   Your learning must take on a new focus. *Be like the little children,* and inhale the world around you in order to make it part of your Self. *Be like the little children,* and learn in order to claim your learning for your Self. Learn who you are through each experience rather than learning in order to find out who you are or what your contribution will eventually be.

30.4   Being in relationship is being present. Being present has nothing to do with time as you think of it. You think of this instruction to be present as an instruction that relates to time. You think of present time, past time, future time. We have spoken of these modes of *keeping* time as well, but as the word *keeping* illustrates, it is only in your perception that time can be kept.

30.5   You are headed toward what might be called universal consciousness, though you will not know it when it is at first achieved. For universal consciousness is knowing Self, while you think it is knowing all. Knowing Self is knowing all, but this you do not as yet understand.

30.6   Universal consciousness is being in relationship. It is the true Self, the *known* Self, in all its glorious relationship with life. All matter is born and dies. All life is forever. The known Self realizes this and begins to act in accordance with this knowing.

30.7   This world as you perceive of it is built around the foundation of fear, a fear that stemmed from the belief in finite life, in being born into a body and dying to the body. The person who *knows,* truly *knows,* the simplest truth of the identity of the Self no longer lives in a dualistic position with God, but in a monistic state with Him. The difference is in realizing relationship with the infinite instead of the finite, with life as opposed to matter.

This huge difference is easily overlooked and rarely seen as the key that unlocks the door to universal consciousness, being present. There is no *being* and no *present* inherent in matter. In matter, being must be attached to form. In the sense of time described by the word *present,* there is no infinitude, but only a vague concept of *now.* This is the key concept that I not only knew but demonstrated. This is the legacy, the inheritance, I left to you.   30.8

This discourse may seem to have traveled far from words of love, words promised and words given in truth. For no love is finite in nature. Love has no beginning and no end. Love is a demonstration and a description of universal consciousness, of being in relationship.   30.9

All relationship is relationship with God Who Is Love.   30.10

What the Course is speaking of now, in essence, is gain without loss. You will never be aware of gain without loss while you believe in what is finite in nature. The cycle of giving and receiving is thus never complete, and the certainty you seek always waiting for something you do not yet have — some information, some guarantee, some proof or validation. You might think if you are "right" you will be successful, if you are "successful" you will be secure, if you are "good" you will prosper. You do not see these ways of thinking as ideas associated with gain and loss, but they are. All thinking that is of an "if this, then that" nature is thinking in terms of gain and loss. This is why we have worked to leave thinking behind. This belief in gain and loss is a cornerstone of your system of perception viewed   30.11

from a stance of "if this, then that." It rules the nature of your existence because you have made it ruler by abandoning the laws of God.

30.12   The laws of God are laws of love. Within the laws of love there is no loss, but only gain.

30.13   The Source of love and its location is your own heart. Think now of the created form, the body. When the heart stops beating, life is seen to be over. Are you thus your heart? Or can you not see that the created form was made in God's own image, as was all creation. You are God's image given form, as is all creation. We, all of us together, are the heartbeat of the world. Without unity we would not be. Without our Source, which is God, we would not be.

30.14   The laws of unity are God's laws and are simple indeed: giving and receiving are one. And thus giving and receiving as one is the only way in which God's laws are fulfilled. Since God's laws are the laws that rule the universe, they cannot go unfulfilled. Giving and receiving are thus one in truth. God's laws are generalizable and do not change, and thus the laws of man have not usurped the laws of God. It is only in your perception that the laws of man take precedence over the laws of God. Since perception arises from the mind, we must now discuss the mind.

CHAPTER **31** | the NATURE
of the MIND

*W*hat you keep you lose. This
is the principle of giving and receiving that, being
finally and totally understood, will free you to be
wholehearted. — 31.14

There is only one Mind, just as there is only one Will. This 31.1
you are afraid of, as you believe this statement threatens your
independence, something you consider a state of being to be
highly prized. This statement, however, more rightly con-
firms your interdependence and your wholeness.

The idea of sharing one heart, one heartbeat, one love, is 31.2
not so unacceptable to you as the idea of sharing one
mind. Your thoughts, you feel, are your own, private and
sacrosanct. These highly guarded and regarded thoughts
are what *A Course in Miracles* calls body thoughts.
Distinctions are made in many religions and philosophies
that separate thought — as dictated by the body — from
thought of a higher order, or spiritual thought. Thoughts
related to your personal self and the "laws" of the body,
such as those of survival, are not the thoughts of the true
Self. This is the clarification that needs to be made for
some of you to fully let go of your fear of the shared
thought system of unity.

31.3   How silly is it to be afraid of the truth? Fear of the truth is like a fear of the impossible being possible. Like the fear of death, it is the product of upside-down thinking.

31.4   You do not understand that something can be inseparable and still not be the same. The miracle of turning water into wine illustrates, as all miracles do, the fallacy of this concept. You must understand this and all miracles correctly if you are to be a miracle worker. What is inseparable cannot be different, but this does not mean it must be the same. Inseparable does not mean replaceable. Water does not replace wine nor wine water, yet each is from the same Source, and so they are not different even while they are not the same.

31.5   Your fear of sameness is your fear of oneness, and it is an unfounded fear, though understandable given your concept of what is the same and what is different. Yet, as your forms so readily illustrate, while all bodies are the same, they are also different. Form but imitates content.

31.6   This is the difficulty with studying the mind. The mind is your being and so you can study it not, no more than you can ever see the entirety of your body unaided, or remove your own brain to view it beneath a microscope. Yet you call your body your own and identify it as your self. Your body moves and breathes, your heart beats and your blood flows, quite unaided by your conscious self. You know that if you had to consciously cause these functions to take place, you would surely die, for managing the workings of the body would be more than your conscious mind could handle. You could not possibly give all the commands necessary if such commands were needed. Thankfully, you have a brain that fulfills this function, yet this brain is also you. Does it work independently from you? Is it separate? Is it the same?

So too is it with mind. Mind *is* your being. It is no acci- 31.7
dent that it has become synonymous to many of you with
brain, an interchangeable word that conveys the same idea.
Mind is the control center, that which remembers and
stores away knowledge, that which is both you and beyond
your understanding of you. Form mimics content. Form
mimics the truth, but does not replace it.

The rest of your world imitates truth as well. You live on 31.8
one world, one planet, one Earth. You may live on different continents, in different countries, various cities, but all
of you rely on the one Earth as part of a sameness and
interdependence you accept. You are aware that this Earth
rests in a cosmos beyond your comprehension, and that
the cosmos too is something that the Earth and all on the
Earth are part of. You believe fully that you are inseparable
from the Earth, the cosmos, gravity, the laws that rule the
universe, just as you believe your brain and, erroneously,
your mind, is inseparable from your body.

Thus your confusion is also your key to understanding. You 31.9
need but look at creation's projection to understand the
nature of perfection and your own Self as creator and created. Being part of the whole that is your known universe
has made you and no other being less consequential. All over
the world people of good faith fight to save even one life.
Each life is irreplaceable and no one argues this point,
yet you allow yourself to resist the whole idea of God
because you believe that what is one cannot also be many.

Give up this notion of losing your Self to God, and you 31.10
will be done for all time with resisting God. Only in God
can you find your Self. This is known to you, and is the
reason for man's quest for God throughout all time. Man
may think he looks to God for answers, for release from

pain, for reward, or for an afterlife. But man has always looked to God for his own Self. Not looking to God to find your Self would be akin to searching everywhere *but* the Earth for humankind. If you do not seek where what you wish to find can be found, you seek in vain.

31.11   The purpose of the mind is extension. Thus, the upside-down perception that causes you to protect your private thoughts and see them as the seat of your self calls for the exact opposite of extension. This is the only true source of conflict. And, yet again, your perception of your thoughts as your self is the closest answer to the truth that you were able, in your limited view of your self, to come up with. There is a part of you that *knows* that you have higher thoughts, and knows that these higher thoughts *are* your Self. Rather than discriminating between higher and lower thoughts, you have aggrandized all your thoughts and given them an identity we have called the ego. Without dislodging your belief in your ego as your self you will never realize your true identity.

31.12   For some this dislodging occurs by coming to a better understanding of the mind, for others by coming to a better understanding of the heart, or love. How the ego becomes dislodged matters not. What matters is where you place your devotion.

31.13   Devotion cannot be split and must be total to be at all. Thus while you believe you are devoted to the thoughts of a split mind you are devoted to nothing. This is why so many attempts at understanding fail. Trying to come to understanding with a split mind is impossible. Impossible learning goals lead to depression. This is why we must learn anew with a mind and heart joined in wholeheartedness.

The ego is that part of yourself that clings to the idea of   31.14
separation, and thus cannot grasp the basic truth of your
existence: that giving and receiving are one in truth. Put
another way, all this says is that in order to *be* your Self,
you have to *share* your Self. What you keep you lose. This
is the principle of giving and receiving that, being finally
and totally understood, will free you to be wholehearted.

All that you would keep private and unshared is, in   31.15
essence, who you think you are. I say who you think you
are because it is important to distinguish who you *think*
you are from who you truly are. On the one hand, you
think that you are your past, your shame, your guilt; on the
other that you are your future, your glory, your potential.
You neither want to share your most negative nor your
most positive thoughts about yourself. These are your great
secrets, the secrets that fill your mind day-to-day with
thoughts that *keep* you from your Self.

And so there is just a small portion of yourself you share,   31.16
the portion that your ego has deemed safe, acceptable, pre-
sentable. The portion that your ego has deemed will cause
you no risk. It is the ego that asks: Are you certain that
if you share that feeling, you will still be loved? Are you certain that if you reveal that secret, you will still be safe? Are
you certain that if you try something new, you will still be
accepted? It is the ego that deems honesty a game; the ego
that you let decide upon your truth. For what you live is
what you believe is the truth about yourself. While you
continue to live dishonestly, your notion of what your
identity truly is cannot improve.

My dear brothers and sisters, what you truly are cannot be   31.17
improved upon. But because you are in a state of unre-
membering, you must relearn who you are. You can only

relearn who you are by being who you are. You can only be who you are by sharing who you are.

31.18   The truth is your identity. Honesty is being free of deception. You, who are already worrying about honesty and sharing being about some need to confess, think a moment about why you are worried. The idea of confessing is an idea of sharing. Rather than thinking of who you are being all tied up with sin and a need for forgiveness, think of this simply as a need to share. This would seem antithetical with what I have already said — that what you keep you lose, and what you share you gain. You think of confessing as a way of letting go and getting rid of that which you do not want. Some of you believe this can be done and others don't. Those who believe in it believe in sin, and that it can be replaced by forgiveness. Those who do not believe in it do not believe that sin can be forgiven and do not seek forgiveness, believing forgiveness is something that they do not deserve. Few truly believe in atonement or undoing. Few truly believe there is no sin. Few truly believe that they are not the sum of their behaviors. How, then, is confession good for the soul?

31.19   You cannot be honest while you do not know the truth about yourself. If you remembered your Self, notions such as confession being good for the soul would be no more. But in order to remember your Self, you need a means of learning who you are. Everything that has ever happened in your life has happened as a learning device to help you remember who you are. Those things about which you feel guilt and shame are simply the remnants of lessons unlearned. While you hang on to them by keeping them hidden, no learning occurs.

31.20   Who you are is love, and all things brought to love are seen in a new light, a light that keeps what you would learn to help you remember who you are, and in that remembrance transforms the rest, leaving you with nothing to be ashamed of, nothing to keep hidden, leaving you with nothing but the truth of who you are. Thus, what you give through sharing you gain *in truth*. No other type of gain is possible.

The same is true of your potentials, which brought to love are accomplished and simply become the truth that has always existed about who you are.   31.21

Sharing is thus not about who you think you are, but about who you truly are, and yet it is the way to learn the difference while learning is still necessary.   31.22

Sharing is the means through which the holy relationship you have with everything is revealed *in truth*. This truth lies within everything that exists, as it lies within you. As you learn that who you are is love, no deception is possible, and you can only be who you are *in truth*.   31.23

What you gain *in truth* is never lost or forgotten again, because it returns remembrance to your mind. What your mind remembers cannot *not* be shared.   31.24

Your ego thoughts can never share the truth with you nor with anyone else. The ego invented the idea of "telling" the truth and using it as an opposite to telling an untruth or lie. Thus were born ideas of being able to keep truth a secret, one of the most ridiculous ideas of the ego thought system.   31.25

Your past has nothing to do with the truth about who you are, except in the degree to which it has or has not helped you to remember who you are. What you have learned *in truth* resides in your mind as a part of you. What you have   31.26

not yet learned from awaits your learning — or in other words, awaits the transfer of your feelings and experience to truth, and thus to your mind. Only the truth abides within your mind, for only it can enter the holy altar you share with me.

31.27 This altar is not a thing, but a devotion to the one truth, the whole truth. Being of one mind is being of one truth, and how can you be of anything less? Only the ego sprang from a lie, the lie of separation that created the illusion of separate minds and varying degrees of truth.

31.28 Just as you look to God for your Self, knowing not what it is you seek, so too do you look to your brothers and sisters and all else that lives along with you. But when you look, knowing not what you seek, what you find varies. Since there is only one truth, finding a variety of answers means nothing. If you but change what you look for, what you see and what you learn will also change.

31.29 If you can look for your Self within your brothers and sisters, however, they must also be able to look for their Selves in you. If you are constantly reflecting back what you think your brothers and sisters want to see, they can learn nothing from you. If the truth about who you think you are changes day-to-day, you are reflecting the very variety of answers they expect to find and have been finding elsewhere.

31.30 You do not think you are looking for yourself in others, but think instead that you are looking for something or someone other than yourself. At certain times of your life you state this seeking you are doing quite clearly, and it is always specific. You are looking for a friend, a spouse, a mentor. You believe you are seeking something other than you to complete yourself, because you *are* seeking to complete yourself. You are seeking wholeness. And you are even correct in seeking it from your brothers and sisters — just not in the way you perceive of it.

When you find the truth of any brother or sister, you find the truth about your Self, for the truth does not change. And if who you truly are *is* the truth, how can you be different? Thus it can be said that the truth and the mind are one in truth. The truth is what is. What is not the truth is illusion. Does this not make perfect sense? 31.31

It is in this perfect sense of the perfect sanity of truth that salvation lies. Salvation is simply your return to your Self. 31.32

If your sister and brother seek the truth, or salvation, from you, and you seek the truth or salvation from them, what is truly occurring? How can this work? This is but another aspect of giving and receiving being one in truth. Giving and receiving are both taking place, both at the same time, as are seeking and finding, once you are aware of what it is you seek. 31.33

This aspect of giving and receiving as one is called relationship. It allows you to experience who you are and thus to know, or remember, who you are. It is in your recognition of the truth about your brother and sister that you recognize the truth about your Self. It is only in relationship that this occurs, because only in relationship are you experiencing anything. 31.34

You do not exist outside of relationship, just as your mind does not exist outside of oneness. Your experience here is but an extension of mind into a realm in which experience 31.35

can occur. Your ego has made of this something different than it is. Rather than extension of mind, your experience has become a projection of ego. This can change.

31.36   As you interact with your brothers and sisters, you seek to get to know them. You do this so that you find what you have in common, and go on from there to shared experiences. You also seek to know your brothers and sisters so that you will come to know what to expect from them. Once you have determined a brother's or sister's usual mode of behavior, deviations from that usual mode concern you. You may determine someone is in a "mood," and see that the effects of that mood are either good or bad, for either you or them or both. Since you live in a world of such extreme uncertainty, one of your highest requirements of those you have relationships with is a mode of behavior that allows you to know what to expect. Thus, as you move from acquaintances to relationships of a deeper nature, you quickly determine the nature of those relationships and have an investment in them staying the same. Since this is most often true for them as well, you too become locked into the expected sameness.

31.37   One relationship in which this is not the case is the relationship of teacher and student. Another relationship that expects change and growth is that of parent to child. These two relationships have comprised your ideas of our Father and me as you have realized that you are here to learn. Now, with a clear learning goal in mind, these idealized relationships must be broadened so that they are seen in *all* rather than in a few, and so that they are seen clearly as what they really are.

32

LOVE RETURNED to LOVE

Thus we end this Course with love given and love received in truth. You are the learner here until you realize that you are Love. You then become the teacher of what you are. Your mind and heart join in wholeheartedness in the embrace. You are home, and there you will forever stay.

— 32.3

Let us first consider the roles of teacher and learner. A   32.1
teacher is first and foremost anything that aids your remembering. Thus look not at the form in which a teacher arrives. It can truly be said that all of life is your teacher. There is not one aspect of it that is not designed to help you to remember who you are. As we have stated repeatedly, the form of your world in many ways reflects the content of who you are. It also reflects the content of who you are not. It is in telling the difference between the two that you need guidance. You have previously looked to those who do not know the difference for your answers. Now you can see that you need to look to a different Source.

That Source is Love, and it is available in every situation but   32.2
for the asking: What would love have me do? What would love have me see? What would love have me say? When you call upon Love you call upon your Source. When you seek the wisdom of your heart you call upon me. When you seek the truth that is in your mind, you call upon the Holy Spirit. Thus is the Sacred Trinity always available in

every situation, and for whichever learning mode you are most comfortable. All learning modes, however, will eventually return you to the Source, which is Love. The difference between Father, Son, and Holy Spirit is but the same difference of which we speak when we assure you that you are of one Mind and one Heart, and that you will not, in coming to know and experience this, lose your Self. The way in which you experience relationship with each aspect of the Trinity is different despite the oneness of the Trinity. The same is true of all relationship with everything. The way in which you experience relationship with each aspect of creation is different despite the oneness of creation. It is in the different relationship of one aspect of creation with all the rest that the difference you so prize as your uniqueness exists. And only there. Only in relationship are you uniquely you. Only relationship exists. For Love *is* relationship.

32.3   Thus we end this Course with love given and love received in truth. You are the learner here until you realize that you are Love. You then become the teacher of what you are. Your mind and heart join in wholeheartedness in the embrace. You are home, and there you will forever stay.

32.4   And thus I say to you, Amen. You have returned to Love, and your relationship with Love has returned you to your Self. Think not. This Course requires no thought and no effort. There is no prolonged study and the few specific exercises are not required. This Course has succeeded in ways you do not yet understand and have no need to understand. These words have entered your heart and sealed the rift between your mind and heart. Be true to love and you cannot fail to be true to your Self.

32.5   If you do not think you are yet prepared, if you think you are not yet ready, cease to think. Read again these words of love and let the sound of love soothe your worries away. Give to me the thoughts that remain to trouble you and I will return them to you transformed by Love. Do not grieve your thoughts or believe in loss of anything of any kind. Thus will all you have already received be remembered in this time of the second coming of Christ.

And what of miracles? The last and final miracle has 32.6 occurred, for what miracles are needed when mind and heart are one and you have returned to the embrace? This is the miracle to end all need of miracles, the only accomplishment of the only Son of God. For what your heart has shared with your mind is shared with all minds and what your heart has to share is only Love. Thus has Love returned to Love.

ADDENDUM: LEARNING in the
TIME OF CHRIST

A year or so after the Course of Love series was complete, Jesus provided "Learning in the Time of Christ" as an aid to those questioning how to work with the material of this Course. It has been edited here to serve as an introduction for taking, and living, A Course of Love. The full text is available from www.acourseoflove.com.

$\mathcal{A}$ major difference between *A Course in Miracles* and *A Course of Love* has to do with the movement into the Time of Christ, a time of direct learning in union and relationship with God. The word "learning" is loosely used here for no learning is needed in union and relationship.

As your work with *A Course of Love* begins, learning and unlearning continue. They continue for the sole purpose for which learning has always existed — that of returning you from self-doubt to self-love. This could also be expressed as returning you from your perceived state of separation to your true state of union. Learning is needed only until perception is cured. The perception of your separated state was the illusion for which a cure was needed . . . and within *A Course in Miracles* offered.

Perception is the result of learning. Perception *is* learning.

Since the mind is the realm of perception we have taken a step away from the realm of perception by appealing to the heart and the heart's ability to "learn" in a new way. You are thus instructed not to apply your thought and your effort, your usual means of learning to this Course of Love. This Course is not for the mind but for the heart. It is not a way of thought and effort but a way of feeling, of ease, and of direct relationship.

In the direct relationship achieved in union, no learning is required. Until you have truly recognized unity, you continue to perceive of yourself as a learning being. This is the only reason for this continuation of the course work provided in *A Course in Miracles*. While you continue to put effort into learning what cannot be learned, as you continue to see yourself as a student seeking to acquire what you do not yet have, you cannot recognize the unity in which you exist and be freed from learning forever.

This is not to say that you will find this Course or the end of learning to be easy. Yet it is your difficulty in giving up your attachment to learning through the application of thought and effort that creates the perception of this difficulty. Thus it is said to you to take this Course with as little attachment to your old means of learning as is possible for you. If you do not understand, accept that you do not understand and go on. Listen to the words as if they are spoken to you, for such they are. Listen as you would listen to a friend in conversation. Listen simply to hear what is being said. Listen simply to let the words enter you.

This is recommended for your first reading of the Course.

When you succeed at listening without seeking for understanding, without grasping for meaning, without applying the effort you are used to applying to study, you begin the transformation that is the movement from head to heart and from their separation to their union.

In wholeheartedness then you are ready to return to a second reading of the Course. In wholeheartedness you will find difficulty falling away and understanding arising. You are beginning to know yourself in a new way. You are beginning to know yourself without the perceptions and the judgments of the mind. You are beginning to know yourself as you truly are and you will begin to hear the language of this Course as the language of your own heart.

Now you may feel quite compelled to share your experience of this Course with others. What might you expect to find?

Often you will find a desire to read the Course again — to read it aloud — to hear it spoken. This is a natural desire to let the words of this Course of Love enter you in yet another way — the way of voice. Listen. Respond. Let meaning be revealed.

What you will find yourself accepting through this method is precisely what cannot be taught. What you are learning through this method is precisely what cannot be sought after and attained through your seeking. What you are finding through this method is receptivity. You are coming home to the way of the heart. What you gain by sharing with others is a situation in which you "learn" in unity through the receptivity of the heart.

Am I telling you not to question? Not to enter discussion? I am only telling you to receive before you perceive. I ask you not to receive as one who does not have what another has. This is not a passing on of information that you do not possess. I ask you merely to receive in order to learn receptivity, the way of the heart. I ask you only to pause, to give the mind a rest, to enter a realm foreign to the mind and yet beloved to the heart. I ask you but to give yourself a chance to let the relief of not having another task to apply your effort to fill you. I ask you but to give yourself a chance to forget about approaching this as one more self-improvement exercise, or one more objective to accomplish. Only in this way do you come to realize you are already accomplished.

Through receptivity, what your mind finds difficult to accept, your heart accepts with ease. Now you are ready to question what you must. Now you are ready to hear the answer that arises in your own heart or from the voice of the man or woman sitting next to you. Now you are ready to hear all the voices around you without judgment, to enter discussion without an agenda, to not be so anxious to say what you are thinking that you forget to listen. Now you are ready to let understanding come without the aggressiveness of going out to get it.

You are patient, loving, and kind. You have entered the time of tenderness. You begin to hear what your feelings are saying to you without the interferences and cautions of your thinking mind. You begin to trust, and as you begin to trust you begin to extend who you are. True giving and receiving as one begins to take place. You have entered Holy Relationship.

How do you feel? is a more appropriate question than *What do you think?* The sharing of experience is more appropriate than the sharing of interpretation. The sharing of process is more appropriate than the sharing of outcome. The only correct interpretation is that which comes from your own internal guidance system. There is no correct answer or specific set of beliefs to be adopted. You begin to move beyond the need for shared belief to personal conviction and authority.

Can you be misguided? Is there, in other words, perhaps no "right" answer or correct interpretation, but "wrong" answers and inaccurate interpretations? This is a matter of unity versus separation rather than a matter of right and wrong. In unity and relationship, each will inevitably receive the answer, and come to the understanding, that is "right" for his or her heart.

Those who do not enter unity and relationship cannot be helped, fixed, or shown the inaccuracies of their perceptions. Their perceptions will remain true for them because their minds have told them they are true and their belief in the supremacy of the mind has temporarily overridden the openness of their hearts. The need for some to remain within the teaching and learning situation of "right" and "wrong" answers will be strong. Many will not be dissuaded from the logic that tells them they must work hard to attain anything of value.

Let me be clear. The lack of difficulty in this Course is where its difficulty lies. To give up difficulty for ease is more than some egos are willing to accept. To give up effort for receptivity is more than some can accept. Why? Because it is too difficult. It goes against all you have learned and the nature of the reality in which the mind has functioned. In turning to the heart we seek to bypass this difficulty as much as possible, but each of you will feel it to some degree, the precise degree to which you are incapable of giving up reliance on what you but think has worked for you in the past.

The way of the heart is the way of the Time of Christ. The time of the Holy Spirit has passed. The time of the intermediary is over. The greatest intermediary of all has been the mind. It has stood between you and your own inner knowing, caught in a dream of perception.

Collectively and individually, you have come to a level of frustration with what can be taught that has exceeded its limits. Your readiness is felt as an impatience. Many can ride the wave of this impatience to a new way. Others need to battle against it a while longer.

For those ready for a new way the time of battles has ended. You care to engage in no more debates, care not to be proven right or proven wrong, care not to hear the evidence for this approach or that. You have grown weary of the ways of the mind. You are ready to come home to the way of the heart.

The way of learning in the Time of Christ brings with it a new kind of evidence, an evidence demonstrated clearly and plainly with every willingness to end reliance on the ego-mind and to leave the hell of the separate self behind. What will be demonstrated and shared is the perfect logic of the heart. Abandonment of the old way will not bring forth ruin but will bring instead the wisdom that each one knows she or he has always possessed.

Through receptivity is the wisdom inherent in being who you truly are revealed. Being who you truly are, accepting your true identity, is the goal of this Course and of this beginning level of what I only loosely call a curriculum.

You naturally may wonder what there is left to strive for and in doing so reach again the very difficult transition away from struggle. In unity, perfection is the reality. Your reality is union. No striving for either unity or perfection is necessary. The "answer" for those in need of challenges, is the challenge presented in the call to reside in unity and to express the divinity of your nature through sharing in union and relationship.

This call is addressed further in the work of the Treatises.

Course of Love Publications is dedicated to the materials, individuals, and relationships associated with the Course of Love.

The way of the heart described in this book is often shared in group and private settings. If you would like to provide information about your group, acquire assistance in starting a group, or arrange a presentation, please contact:

Course of Love Publications
432 Rehnberg Place
W. St. Paul, Minnesota 55118
acol@thedialogues.com

The Course of Love series includes:

A Course of Love
The Treatises of A Course of Love
The Dialogues of A Course of Love

The books of the Course of Love are available toll free at 1-800-901-3480, at bookstores by special order, from on-line retailers, or from the following websites:

www.acourseoflove.com
and www.ItascaBooks.com